# Praise for *Whatever the* ......

"Keri Ohlrich and Kelly Guenther have written the kickass motivational book you won't want to put down. Truly insightful (and hilarious), *Whatever the Hell You Want* is the guide that will get you just that. Grab this book and put their direct, relatable, and achievable strategies to use today!"

—**Cara Tuttle,** author, *Drowning in Timidity: Women, Politeness, and the Power of Assertive Living*

"Rarely do you find a book that reads like a practical, human, hilarious guide to meaningful change. This book accomplishes that heady goal and more! I spent most of my time reading thinking that I was tucked into a corner pub with my mentors, and they were telling me all the stuff that I needed to hear, even if it was a tough truth, along with strategies to anticipate and survive the inevitable challenges. When I put the book down, I felt inspired and motivated, which is great; I also felt seen, which is remarkable."

—**Dr. Matthew Zakreski,** licensed clinical psychologist, keynote speaker, adjunct professor

"Ready to break free from societal constraints? *Whatever the Hell You Want* is your guide to reclaiming autonomy in midlife. Kelly and Keri's empowering book offers a road map for shedding outdated roles and pursuing passions with unapologetic fervor. Filled with practical advice and empowering anecdotes, it's a rallying cry for people to live authentically and seize the reins of their destiny."

—**Joli Hamilton, PhD,** relationship coach, TEDx speaker, jealousy expert, research psychologist, professor, author, podcast host

"*Whatever the Hell You Want* by Keri Ohlrich and Kelly Guenther is an extraordinary book that serves as both inspiration and a practical guide for anyone feeling trapped by societal expectations or personal pressures. It beautifully validates the idea that stepping away from the paths laid out by parents, partners, and corporate mandates isn't just possible, but can lead to unparalleled joy and success. This isn't just a book; it's a journey into self-discovery, offering real-life insights and actionable steps to break free from the 'little boxes' that confine us. Whether it's redefining success, carving out a unique professional path, or simply living life on your own terms, Ohlrich and Guenther's combined expertise and personal anecdotes make for a compelling and relatable guide. I wholeheartedly recommend this book to anyone looking to reclaim their life. It's a reminder that the permission to do Whatever the Hell You Want comes from within, and that happiness and authenticity are within reach when we dare to chase them."

—**Amy Kavanaugh Mason,** cofounder, Candified Inc.;
former chief engagement officer, Taco Bell;
chief marketing officer, Dine Brands International

"This book is a game-changer! I wish I had it when summoning the courage to leave my marriage and job simultaneously. It captures the essence of genuine change, blending desire with action. With a mix of humor, inspirational tales, and practical methods, it serves as the ultimate guide for embracing both 'doing and being.' This handbook is a treasure trove for anyone seeking lasting change to shape a truly fulfilling life. If you're ready to embark on a transformative journey, this book is your compass!"

—**Lyndal Larkin,** executive coach, leadership advisor,
founder and principal, Larkin Leadership

"The charm mixed with dangerous honesty here is really refreshing. In many ways, it feels like the tough love talk we've all been waiting for, acknowledging where we fall short and hoping and pushing us to do better. We read several chapters as a family and talked about it for days afterwards. Highly recommend."

—**Sean Daniels,** writer, director, advocate

"An honest and unfiltered journey that will inspire anyone to shed the weight of expectations and discover how it's not only possible, but enviable, to live an authentic life. Keri and Kelly share deeply personal stories and provide simple tools to show how anyone can use humor and self-reflection to find your best self."

—**Jennifer Turner,** president and CEO,
Tennessee Performing Arts Center

"This book resonates deeply with me, as I have experienced numerous twists and turns in my own life. It emphasizes the importance of living authentically as the ultimate solution. With its step-by-step guide and easy-to-understand concepts, it provides a road map to break free from the confines of societal expectations and embrace true self-expression."

—**Madeline Borkin,** vice president of membership, executive sponsor of i4cp Chief Diversity Officer board

"For those looking for a supportive, uplifting, and motivational journey toward carving out your own unique path to happiness and doing it on your own terms, your search is over! Keri and Kelly through their personal knowledge of breaking through expectations, have created a powerful read that allows readers to define expectations from which they want to break free, while doing so in a way that is truly at their pace. Their commitment to empowering us to live our best lives radiates from each page— and celebrates each step along the way."

—**Sharon Armstrong,** best-selling coauthor of *The Essential HR Handbook*

"A refreshingly authentic approach to uncovering the root of expectations, challenging cognitive biases, and facilitating a journey toward a life grounded in values. Keri and Kelly's combined wisdom and candid perspectives on self-expectation pave the way for purposeful shifts toward a values-centered life. *Whatever the Hell You Want* is a manual for mastering the art of questioning norms and dissecting expectations, ultimately shattering the boundaries we confine ourselves within. Join Keri and Kelly on a delightful journey to uncover the expectations holding you back as they bring humor and insight to embracing a life rooted in values."

—**Hilary S. Lyn, MS, MA,** president, Association for Women in Communications, Santa Barbara; Fielding Graduate University Social Innovation Fellow; founder, Pivot and Rise Coaching and Consulting

"In this candid and empowering book, Keri and Kelly dismantle the little boxes that confine us and offer a blueprint for living a life that is truly our own. An unapologetic celebration of freedom, choice, and authenticity, *Whatever the Hell You Want* will inspire you to redefine success on your terms."

—**Ashley Jordan,** author, *Unhappy Achiever*

"Drawing on the lived experiences of authors individually, who share the evolution of their friendship and how they came to be strong business-women and podcasters, *Whatever the Hell You Want* invites us to challenge the inherited, limiting beliefs women may have subconsciously retained."

—**Lizbeth Meredith,** podcaster, award-winning author of *Pieces of Me* and *Grounded in Grit: Turn Your Challenges into Superpowers*

"*Whatever the Hell You Want* stands as a beacon of hope for those seeking to break free from the confining boxes that life often thrusts upon us. You will find not just a book, but a manifesto—a call to arms for individuals tired of conforming to others' standards and yearning to embrace their true selves.

Through a blend of wisdom, humor, and unapologetic honesty, this book serves as your guide to dismantling the barriers that hold you back and stepping boldly into the life you've always desired. It's a reminder that you are not defined by the labels others impose upon you, nor are you confined to the roles society assigns. You have the power to chart your own course, pursue your passions, and chase your dreams—whatever the hell they may be. Remember this: you are worthy of a life filled with passion, purpose, and joy. You deserve to pursue whatever the hell you want. Go ahead, flip the page, and let the journey begin."

—**Colonel (Ret.) Charlie Davis,** CEO, Davis Strategic Consulting and Coaching

# Whatever the Hell You Want

# Whatever the Hell You Want

## An Escape Plan to Break Out of Life's Little Boxes and Live Free from Expectations

**Keri Ohlrich, PhD & Kelly Guenther**

WONDERWELL

Published by Wonderwell Press
Austin, Texas
www.gbgpress.com

This work is being published under the *Wonderwell Press* imprint by an exclusive arrangement with *Wonderwell*. *Wonderwell*, *Wonderwell Press*, and the *Wonderwell* logos are wholly-owned trademarks of *Wonderwell*.

Distributed by Greenleaf Book Group

For ordering information or special discounts for bulk purchases, please contact Greenleaf Book Group at PO Box 91869, Austin, TX 78709, 512.891.6100.

Design and composition by Greenleaf Book Group
Cover design by Adrian Morgan

Publisher's Cataloging-in-Publication data is available.

Print ISBN: 978-1-963827-04-0

eBook ISBN: 978-1-963827-05-7

To offset the number of trees consumed in the printing of our books, Greenleaf donates a portion of the proceeds from each printing to the Arbor Day Foundation. Greenleaf Book Group has replaced over 50,000 trees since 2007.

Printed in the United States of America on acid-free paper

24 25 26 27 28 29 30 31   10 9 8 7 6 5 4 3 2 1

First Edition

*This book is dedicated to the courageous souls prepared to live life on their own terms. As you embark on this transformative journey, know that we are with you, supporting you with our love, humor, and motivation. This isn't just a dedication; it's a promise of unwavering support. So, as you navigate the twists and turns ahead, remember: You've got this!*

# Contents

Introduction     1

**PART I:** Be Brave and Realize Your Expectations     11

Chapter 1: Introducing BREAK     13

Chapter 2: Okay, Freud, You Were Right about Our Parents     33

Chapter 3: OMG. Yep, Those Religious Expectations     59

Chapter 4: Boys Will Be Boys, But Just Be a Good Girl     71

Chapter 5: Where You Came From Matters     93

Chapter 6: Don't Worry—
You Will Find a Nice Person to Marry     111

Chapter 7: Nice to Meet You! What Do You Do?     137

**PART II:** Explore, Take Action, and Keep It Going!     153

Chapter 8: What the Hell Do You Really Want?     155

Chapter 9: Time to Take Action:
Break Out of Your Boxes Like a Champion     175

Chapter 10: Keep It Going and Live Free!     187

Acknowledgments     201

Bibliography     205

Notes     211

About the Authors     219

# Introduction

*Fuck the expectations.*

There—we said it. (And we'll say it a few more times before we're done.)

As coaches, change experts, and talent specialists fascinated by human transformation, we started our podcast, *The Breakout*, to discover the different ways that people have successfully created lives on their own terms. What they told us again and again was that forging their own path meant giving unwanted expectations the big middle finger.

Each found themselves at a pivotal moment when they could either choose to stay stagnant or embrace the lives they were meant to be living. To make that change, they first had to buck the expectations that stood in their way.

Whose expectations are we talking about? They might be those of our parents, our partner, our friends, our religion, society as a whole . . . and even expectations we put on ourselves. Expectations that dictate how we act, what we say, where we go, what we do, what we wear, who we love, and certainly what we're "allowed" to accomplish in life. Expectations that often keep us locked in a tight little box labeled, "No, you can't" or "Stop! You shouldn't!" or "You don't have the right" or "You'd never pull *that* off." Or worse yet, "You aren't good enough."

But here's the thing: Expectations are not the same as obligations. It can feel like an expectation is an absolute truth—something that you must fulfill no matter what. But if you look at it more closely, you will no doubt discover that it isn't an absolute truth at all. You are not obligated to fulfill anyone else's expectations of you if you don't want to. You don't have to marry anyone or even date to have plenty of love in your life. You don't have to hold a nine-to-five job or be a world-traveling influencer to produce meaningful work. And you sure as hell don't have to wear the latest trends because they are in style. You don't *have to*, but you definitely can if you *want to*.

You're not alone if you've encountered expectations from your family, friends, teachers, bosses, society at large, and yourself for how you *should* look, the type of person you *should* be, and the work you *should* do. But at the end of the day, *it's your life*, and this book is your permission slip to do and be *whatever the hell you want*.

In a world that's telling you no, we are telling you *yes*.

We're passionate about the opportunity to live fully, and we'd love nothing more than to see everyone break out from the expectations that have kept them trapped in a life that doesn't serve them.

Recognizing the ways in which we've allowed expectations to rule our lives and dictate our decisions isn't always immediately obvious, however. It requires a de-conditioning, a clearing away of old, fractured beliefs, and a new model for creating a life by your design—and that is exactly what we are here to help you do.

Take a moment to consider the quality of your own thoughts. When was the last time you were in the process of making a choice, big or small, from what to do next in your career to what to make for dinner, and a thought stopped you in your tracks?

*"I can't go back to school; I'm too old to start a new career."*

*"I'm giving my kids frozen dinner again; I'm a bad parent."*

*"I'm thirty-five and still not married; maybe there is something wrong with me."*

*"I can't get a divorce. It will mess the kids up, and they will grow to hate me."*

These internal scripts about what your choices say about you as a person came from somewhere. At the root of many of our biggest self-limiting beliefs are the expectations that others and we ourselves have accepted as rules for how to live. Yet, each of these predetermined invisible rules affects our day-to-day lives, challenges our self-worth, and slowly but surely keeps us from pursuing our dreams and being our whole and complete selves.

Maybe you still aren't sure if or how expectations have stood in your way, but you recognize that you feel stuck, stifled, suffocated, stressed, or at least dissatisfied with some aspect of your life. Perhaps you feel like you never get to do what you want or that your talents aren't being used or expressed in ways that you'd prefer. Or do you have ideas that you never manage to implement? Perhaps there's a hobby you'd like to explore but are afraid of what your friends or partner might think. Maybe you're in a job that's highly competitive and sought after, but you just don't enjoy it. Or do you feel doomed to have a boring life? Do you feel like you're living a life that was pre-scribed for you? You might not know what's wrong exactly, but you know you feel stressed out and restricted. Something's just plain "off."

If you identify with this, you are far from alone. Adam Alter, the author of *Anatomy of a Breakthrough*, conducted a survey in which 70 percent of the respondents said they could easily think of an area of their life where they felt stuck, and 50 percent said they had been stuck for years or decades.[1]

The United States may still be the wealthiest country in the world, but even before the COVID-19 pandemic, the World Happiness Report found that Americans ranked only sixteenth among the happiest nations.[2]

Of course, it's one thing to have a vague sense we aren't happy. It's quite another to know why or what to do about it. You might be saying to yourself, "Okay, fine. Maybe I'm living in a little box and letting expectations hold me back, but I don't even *know* what the hell I want." We get that.

In fact, that is what this book is all about. Our goal is to help you discover what you truly want, break out of the little boxes, and discard the false beliefs that aren't serving you so that you can finally *live* this one life you've been given. Stop for a second to just consider how powerful that is! *(And pardon us while we tear up. This topic always gets us right in the heart because making the most of your life means everything!)*

## WHO THE HELL ARE WE, AND WHY SHOULD YOU LISTEN TO US?

The two of us met thirteen years ago while working for the same company in Wisconsin and have been best friends since. In that time, we've watched each other go through a *lot* of changes.

Keri hired Kelly and that is how the bond began! "We quickly developed a deep trust and respect for each other. Plus, we have so much fun together!" Kelly says. "We're so different, but we complement each other well. Keri is the big-picture thinker who's a great influencer and rule-breaker, while I'm more about the details, the process, and the structure. It makes for a great partnership!"

After a while, Keri got a job in Southern California and moved there with her husband and son. In a strange coincidence, Kelly was also offered a change management role in Southern California about six months later.

It felt great to be in the same city again. Our friendship no longer had to be restricted to phone calls and Zoom chats.

As it turned out, however, even though we liked California, those promising new jobs left a lot to be desired. We both felt constrained by the corporate machine, which felt like quite a tiny box to squeeze into. We didn't feel free to be our true selves, and everything moved at a snail's pace, preventing us from making any real impact in the Human Resources field. We admit that we groveled in our misery for more than a minute, grumbling to each other, "I can't believe we have to contact recruiters again!" Yes, we bonded over tears. And realistically, we had to concede that most companies would probably suffer from the same issues we'd already muddled through—uncomfortable corporate politics and an aversion to creative thinking, just to name two. How much of ourselves would we have to suppress in order to fit into the corporate mold?

The answer was staring us right in the face, but frankly, neither of us ever thought we'd start our own business. The prospect was damn scary. But it was even scarier to think we might get stuck again in the little boxes that corporate job expectations would require of us. To add to the mix, we had naysayers in our lives with their own doomsday predictions:

*"Rents in southern California are sky high, so if you aren't successful, you'll be screwed!"*

*"You'll never make any money."*

*"It'll destroy your friendship, and you won't be besties anymore. Friends should never go into business together!"*

*"You'll be ruined, and you'll struggle to get a corporate job again when your business tanks."*

Lots of people treated us like we were boarding the *Titanic*. But by that point, we'd both been around long enough to know these people were just expressing their own fears. We didn't need that—we had enough of our own, thank you very much. Luckily, we had also learned how to put our fears aside enough to take action.

Of course, we knew starting a business would be a real risk, but we also knew that nothing amazing happens without risk. Despite the high rents, Southern California is also a big market. We both have an incredible work ethic, so we figured whatever odds might be against us, we still had plenty of good odds in our favor. Plus, our friendship and loyalty toward one another felt like our ace in the hole.

Seven years later, we are proud to say we work with individuals as coaches and still run Abbracci Group together, our boutique consulting firm driven by a mission to empower organizations, leaders, teams, and individuals to unlock their full potential for transformative and sustainable growth. We haven't lost our shirts, our friendship is stronger than ever, and we're no longer confined to a box.

I (Keri) now cannot believe that I would ever *not* have a company with Kelly. I don't have biological siblings, but I now have a sister. It's the best feeling in the world! There isn't anything we wouldn't do for each other.

We are iPEC Certified Professional Coaches (CPC) and Prosci®-certified change management practitioners. We understand how change works. Together, we have successfully implemented high-level change management models that worked beautifully in a variety of business environments, and we have coached individuals to break out of their own stuffy boxes due to unwanted expectations.

Prosci conducted a study which found that 93 percent of organizations that implemented excellent change management programs (programs that exceeded objectives in each of the change management effectiveness categories) said they "met or exceeded project objectives."[3] With those kinds of results, we started to think, *Why can't these models we've seen work over and over in companies also work for individuals in their personal lives? Prosci combined with our individual coaching can be a winning combination.*

It turns out they can! In fact, when we looked back at what's worked for each of us in our own lives, for people we have coached, and for people we've interviewed on our podcast, we saw our change models in action. Applying the same method we have seen work time and time again, we will walk you through the practical steps to break out of your own boxes and create the life you want.

After more than twenty years of coaching people on this topic, we understand the expectations that people place on themselves as well as the expectations that are placed on them. For all these reasons, we need proven strategies for fucking the expectations if we're going to be who we want to be and live the life we choose. That's the whole point of this book. It's the difference between sleepwalking through your life and engaging passionately with it. Which would you rather do?

Yeah, we thought so.

The bottom line is that we believe in telling the status quo to suck it. We support anyone who desires to live a life defined by their own values. With self-awareness comes the knowledge of who you are, what you want, what you *don't* want, and the courage to make the decisions needed to live the best version of your life. You just need the right tools, information, and guidance. And now you've picked up the right book.

## HERE'S YOUR ESCAPE PLAN

Fair warning: We aren't going to sugarcoat anything. Some of these chapters will go deep. Challenging the status quo is . . . well, challenging. But as you continue reading, you'll learn more and more that letting go of expectations and living on your own terms is so, so worth it.

You may find yourself moving easily through some of the chapters, while you might want to skip others because they feel too painful to handle. We ask that you read all of them because you just never know what you'll discover there. The shiniest gold for you may be in a chapter that doesn't seem worth the discomfort. But take breaks as needed and remember to be gentle with yourself if a chapter brings up difficult emotions.

While we have found that the mechanics of breaking expectations are similar regardless of race, gender, religion, or geographic location, we also want to acknowledge that we are white cisgendered women. While we'll touch on race a bit in this book, we are not experts on this subject. We recognize and acknowledge our privilege and know that the challenges faced by some are far more serious than anything we have had to endure. While we have done our best to become aware of our own biases, we know we may have some that are still unconscious. We suggest that every reader consider and seek out the resources and support that they need as they examine breaking the expectations in their lives.

Each chapter will have a similar rhythm. We will share some stories of people who have been suffocated in their little boxes and some who have busted out to live the lives they were always meant to. We'll also infuse the information with a touch (but just a touch) of research. (I mean, c'mon, Keri did get a PhD!) At the end of each chapter, we'll provide some exercises to prompt you to think about what expectations you have put on yourself, what others have told you, what you want for yourself, and how to make the changes that will make the difference.

If it sounds daunting, remember that we'll be with you as you read every page. After listening to more than one hundred stories on our podcast and countless stories of people we've coached, one of the key things we've learned is that none of us can make big changes in life alone. You must be willing to accept help and support. Through these pages, it's our intent to be that support for you. We hope you'll feel us cheering you on as you absorb each chapter and take the first step toward the life that's waiting for you—a life with the weight of unwanted expectations lifted from your shoulders. A life where there are no walled-in boxes to hold you back. A life of your own design.

# Part I

# Be Brave and Realize Your Expectations

# CHAPTER 1
# Introducing BREAK

Have you ever changed your plans for the day or sacrificed something you wanted to meet someone else's expectations? Have you ever done something just because it's what has "always" been done?

*Of course you have!* At some point (or perhaps at many points), we have all been influenced by our family, friends, partners, community, teachers, social media, and more to be, do, and behave in a certain way. Can't you just hear their voices now? *"You'll go broke if you start your own company!"* *"What? You can't just elope!"* *"Um, aren't you too old to pull off those sequins?"* But we all deserve happiness, security, joy, peace, and to live authentically as ourselves, which can only be achieved when we are living the life we have chosen. And this book is designed to help you live as *you* choose.

In this chapter, we will introduce you to our plan to help you BREAK away from the expectations that have prevented you from making this life what you really want it to be. Expectations that are like little boxes that you have squeezed yourself into (or like pants two or three sizes too small), only to find yourself stuck and unable to move freely, or even breathe. We know exactly what that's like. We, too, have been stuck and have since spent years learning how to break free, while helping others do the same.

We know this path isn't easy. Bucking the status quo can be an uphill battle. While it's true that even at a young age, we both possessed a certain amount of sass (sometimes outright refusing to obey conventions), it hasn't been a walk in the park to always be exactly who we are and do exactly what we want. There have been plenty of times throughout our lives when we struggled to follow our own desires in the face of what others wanted us to do or be.

Becoming change experts and launching our own business didn't happen overnight, either. Identifying what works and why it works took us years of studying and observing hundreds of people as they made intentional changes for the better. Honestly, there's nothing more rewarding than helping people learn how to be truly free. Watching them break out of their boxes is just about the most exciting thing we do!

Still, our very first case studies were *ourselves*. Before we developed the strategies you will read on these pages, we lived them through trial and error.

Our stories are a reminder that choosing to break out of your boxes and live the life you want has nothing to do with being born a rule-breaker or having such a tough skin that you don't care what people think. You can be human, shed as many tears as needed, and still transform your life. Each and every one of us has this ability. For the two of us, it started with one choice we had to make for ourselves, and that we all must make at some point—the choice whether to live our life or someone else's.

# FIRST, WE MUST BELONG TO OURSELVES
## —Kelly

I've hardly been what you'd call a rebel throughout my life. I love schedules, color-coded sticky notes, and having a detailed plan. But even as a kid, I never quite saw life the same way as my family or friends did.

I was in third grade when my cousin got engaged, and while in the car one day, my mother, aunt, and sister discussed the wedding. Everyone started to guess how many kids the newlyweds might have, to which I said, "What if they don't want to have kids?" Everyone in the car went into a state of shock. Of course, my cousin and her husband would have children, they all insisted!

Then, I shocked them even more. "I know I don't want to have kids," I said definitively.

My aunt quickly snapped back, "Well, that's why you were put on this earth."

Talk about a box to get stuck in! My only purpose in life was to procreate? No way. That comment just made me dig in my heels even more. *Now I'm for sure not having kids*, I thought.

In Wisconsin, where I grew up, it was the norm for little girls to say they wanted to be a mommy when they grew up. It felt like everyone was expected to get married and have children. But even as I got older, I remained crystal clear that I didn't want to follow the pack on this, and I've held to that decision all these years later despite the expectations of my extended family and community.

There's certainly nothing wrong with Wisconsin, but I felt suffocated there in many ways, both personally and professionally. It seemed that nearly everyone around me was focused on their babies. They talked about the best strollers on the market, which neighborhoods had the best schools, or whether timeouts worked or not. I couldn't relate, which made it hard to find people in my age group with common interests who were willing to go out for a nice evening (especially since it meant hiring a babysitter). So, when my company offered me a position in California at age thirty-six, I jumped at the opportunity.

There was just one problem. In my family and greater community, you simply didn't move far away from your parents. I assume if I'd been married, and my husband got a job in California, that would have been considered more acceptable. But as a single woman moving to another state clear across the country, no one could understand it. It was yet another little box I was supposed to sit in quietly and dutifully.

When my company offered to relocate me, I thought, "It would be crazy not to do this." I could break out of the box, or I could stay where I was, complaining nonstop for the next twenty years. So, I took a deep breath, said "fuck the expectations," and went west.

After the move, I spent a *lot* of time crying. I was filled with excitement at how refreshing and altogether different California felt—and to reunite with Keri, who had moved to Los Angeles six months before—but I was also deeply heartbroken knowing that my family had doubts. Yet, despite my family's reaction, I knew it was the right thing to do for *me* and what I wanted out of my life.

It took them a long time to get over it, but I'm happy to say that now, they're 100 percent on board. Taking that leap allowed me to start a whole new and exciting phase of my life. I'm so grateful I had the courage to say no to what everyone else thought I *should* do and follow what felt right for me. It led to the founding of my company with Keri and many great adventures that I could have missed.

When I packed and walked away, I had no way of knowing if my parents would ever come around. I'm lucky they did. It's true that sometimes, following our heart can cause others to cut us off. But if I had stayed just to placate them, I would have relegated myself to that little box, feeling like I was wearing a straitjacket. The tendency to shape our lives based on the expectations of others is responsible for a lot of the world's misery. For that reason, I believe the only choice we have is to be ourselves. The alternative is unacceptable.

We all want and need other people to help us feel we belong, but first and foremost, we have to belong to ourselves.

## YOU CAN'T AFFORD TO WAIT
—Keri

In some ways, I have been a natural at turning my back on the status quo. When I was a kid, I brushed off the Brownies troop because they wanted us to pay twenty-five cents for playtime, and I thought that was dumb. "Why should we pay twenty-five cents when members can just come over to my house to play for free?" So, I started my own version of a Brownies troop when I was in second grade. "Join my troop," I said, "and you won't have to pay me anything!" (On second thought, that might have been a missed revenue opportunity.)

You'll also learn more in a later chapter about how I threw tradition out the window when I planned my wedding in Vegas. But I don't want you to think I just came out of the womb ready to give everybody's expectations the finger. I know firsthand that what others expect of us (or what we expect of ourselves) can take a horrible toll.

When I was in my late teens, I was in an enormous amount of emotional pain. My parents had divorced when I was five years old, and I lived with my mother. She had such high expectations of me since she saw any failing on my part as a reflection on her. I had to behave like a miniature version of her or she would be embarrassed. In her mind, any assertion of my own identity invalidated her own choices and self-image. She was disgusted that I didn't like orchestra concerts, and if I got sick, she took it as a reflection on her. "I can't believe you're sick. How will that make me look?" she'd say. She also graded my behavior from A to F, as if she was giving me a report card. At the same time, I felt I was failing to meet the expectations of my father and the new family he had built. I was supposed to just accept the new family without any negative feelings about it because my dad needed that illusion.

All I wanted was to be loved and accepted, but I felt very much alone. By my teen years, the weight of these expectations and my parents' conditional form of love built up my anger to a breaking point.

I wanted to shatter the image that my mother created with her friends and family, so I plotted my suicide. *That will show her*, I thought. And as someone who tends to follow through on goals, I intentionally crashed my car. Afterward I sat inside it, realizing I was barely injured. *Great*, I thought, *nothing will change.*

And nothing did. My parents blamed it all on stress. "She just does too much," they claimed, in complete denial. Meanwhile, I was shamed by my grandparents for being a bad driver. I came out of the hospital feeling just as unlovable as before. Inside, I wanted to scream, telling them all, "I did it on purpose to show you all that your pressure and expectations are bullshit!"

But I didn't. I carried that secret with me, along with the belief that I was unlovable, and I didn't tell anyone until much later in life. At the age of twenty-eight, I finally started dealing with the pain of my upbringing and the expectations that provided me with such a shaky foundation. There were a lot of tears, some heavy drinking, and a hefty amount of avoidance before I finally got enough therapy to help me break out. But I did it. Bye-bye, boxes!

From where I sit now, I'm so grateful I didn't die in that car crash. I would have missed the beautiful life I have today with my husband, son, friends, and my bestie, Kelly. My life is kick-ass because I get to be myself with the people I love most. I finally have the unconditional love I wanted so much as a kid. And this is what propels me to pay it forward. I hate for others to be in the kind of pain I experienced, and I know that far too many people are. I know how many try to mold themselves into what others want. But like Kelly, I've learned that living a lie is an awful life sentence. Breaking out and being who we are might feel difficult in the short term, but in the long term, it gives us the gift of freedom. Ultimately, that's the only way to be truly alive, and I'm just glad I survived and gave myself the opportunity to discover the rewards of being me rather than someone else's picture of me.

My choice to break out of the boxes that others had chosen for me and build a life on my own terms ultimately saved my life, and I'm so glad I didn't wait any longer to do it. Luckily, for most of us, breaking out of our boxes and refusing to abide by unwanted expectations is not quite so dramatic, but it can still be so stifling that we settle for less than the full life we're capable of enjoying. We simply can't afford to wait to find out who we are, what we truly want, or to take action to design our life accordingly. *If the only choice for a full life is to be yourself, then the only time to be unapologetically you is now.*

With that in mind, let's take a look at the process that will serve as your foundation while you walk through these chapters with us.

## THE BREAK METHOD

Throughout this book, you will learn how to identify the little boxes of expectation that have kept you trapped. Then, you will prioritize what you want and map out how to get it. This is how you will finally live a life of unwavering choice and lasting freedom.

To help you get there, we have created a process we call BREAK. Each letter stands for one part of the process that you will follow as you continue reading.

Where did BREAK come from? In our Human Resources jobs, we have followed what are called "organizational change management models." That might sound like a big yawn, but they're actually pretty cool. Even when working with a Fortune 125 company to transform an 1,800-person business delivery model, we discovered that organizational changes are still all about individual *people*. Companies don't change; humans do. So, as we started to work with individuals, worked on transforming our own lives at the same time, and interviewed our many podcast guests, the steps that truly work to help people change and break out of those confining boxes became clearer and clearer. We borrowed a bit from the change models we knew, like those of Dr. John Kotter, Kurt Lewin, and ADKAR (part of the Prosci® model), but our version is all about saying au revoir, sayonara, and adios to the expectations that are between you and the life you deserve. That's how BREAK was born.

### BREAK stands for:

- Brave—be brave enough to think about making a change
- Realize which expectations stand in your way
- Explore the possibilities available to you

- Act to get out of those stuffy boxes
- Keep it going and live free!

Let's talk a bit more about each of these.

The first three letters—B, R, and E—represent the pre-change stage of the process and Part One of the book. The A represents the actual change stage, and the K is the post-change phase. Part 2 of the book will focus on the change and post-change phases.

Whether it's one person or a whole organization, it seems to be human nature to want to jump to the action part, skipping the pre- and post-change bits. After all, that feels like the meatiest segment, doesn't it, where you'll see the most results? But we have learned the hard way that skipping the pre- and post-change stages is a whopper of a mistake because it's difficult to sustain changes without the right kind of preparation. That's why we will spend the most time on the pre-change part. *You simply can't break free of even one expectation without each of these steps.* Let's now look at each letter a little more closely.

**Be Brave Enough to Think About Making a Change.** This first step of pre-change is about taking a deep breath and being brave enough to just *think* about changing. We'll start by asking how you are *really* feeling about the different areas of your life. Do you know you're stressed out or dissatisfied in some ways but have no idea why? In this step, you will begin to take an honest look at where you are *right now* and start to muster up the bravery to think about what needs to happen next.

**Realize the Expectations Standing in Your Way.** This is the step where we really lean in on increasing your awareness of the expectations you have faced in the different areas of your life and the harm they may be causing you. These include family, religion, and various aspects of society. Like peeling an onion, after we've cut to the center, you will have greater self-awareness. And we all need more awareness! Psychologist Tasha Eurich, author of the book *Insight: The Surprising Truth About How Others See Us, How We See Ourselves, and Why the Answers Matter More Than We Think,* conducted a series of surveys and came to the conclusion that 95 percent of us think we're self-aware, but only 10 to 15 percent of us actually are.[1] Yikes! As our podcast guest and Own Your Amazing Coach Dr. Denise Moore Revel told us, "You've got to stop and get to know who you really are—outside of your husband, outside of your kids, outside of your career. Who are you really *for you?* That's the first question, and that's the hardest question for a lot of us to answer." In other words, are you living the life you want for you, or are you trying to be who everyone else wants you to be? That's what you'll answer in this part, and you'll find it has the most chapters of any part of the book because it's just that important!

**Explore the Possibilities Available to You.** It's one thing to realize you have undertaken a career because it's what your parents expected of you, or that you have been restricted under the weight of gender expectations or your religion's requirements. But it's another thing to unravel what you might want instead. This step is when you'll start to think about what truly matters to you. With the expectations taken out of the equation, what the hell do you really want?

**Act to Get Out of Those Stuffy Boxes.** Now, we finally move out of the pre-change phase into the stage everyone wants to jump ahead to. This is when you will devise your escape plan and decide how to make whatever the hell you want a reality. What do you need to *do* to finally be free?

**Keep It Going and Live Free.** As we said, the post-change phase is another one people like to skip, much to their detriment. You'll learn just how easy it is to fall back into old habits and let those confining expectations take over your life again. After all, society is always trying to lock us back up in restrictive boxes, and you probably have some family members who would feel more comfortable with you in an old familiar box. So that means it's up to you to stay free by learning how to reinforce the changes you've made and to sustain your new life. In other words, post-change is all about sticking the landing and living the life you choose for the rest of your days.

That's the plan! We hope you're as excited about it as we are and ready to roll up your sleeves because we want you to roll them up right now.

## BE BRAVE

How many of us sleepwalk through our days, barely even noticing if we've had a single moment of enjoyment? We're so busy filling up the dishwasher, rushing to a meeting with our boss, and fighting with customer service over the cell phone bill that we don't have time to think about what's working in our lives . . . and what isn't. Hey, it's easy to do, and we're all guilty of it at least some of the time.

But before you can figure out what you need to do differently in order to make the most of this life, you've got to STOP and be brave enough to take an inventory of how you feel right now. And we mean *really* stop and give it more attention than just lip service. That's where the bravery really comes in.

You may not even realize yet that in one or more areas of your life, you're sitting in a box so little that your inner badass has no room to play, fight, or maybe even breathe. Let's assess how big or small your life's boxes are from where you sit at this moment.

## THE SQUEEZE

In the following exercise, you'll look at a few key areas of your life and ask yourself just how boxed in you feel. These areas include your family of origin, your religion/spiritual background, your community, love/marriage, and your career/work life. How do you know if you're stuck in a box? Do you feel burned out, stressed, dissatisfied, or like you aren't free to be yourself in this aspect of your life? We believe that your level of satisfaction is likely to correlate with the number of unwanted expectations that you face in that aspect of your life. So, for each one, we have created an image that represents the little boxes you might find yourself stuffed inside.

You are sitting in the center. For each, you'll choose one of the following:

SMALL is for the areas of your life where you feel super-duper boxed in—suffocated and crushed by the walls closing in on you. If this is the case, you're sure this aspect of your life isn't working, even if you have no idea why yet.

MEDIUM is when you feel pretty boxed in but are still handling your shit. This box isn't as small as the previous one. You have a little more breathing room, but at the same time, you're stressed out. This part of your life isn't exactly making you want to dance to your favorite song even if, again, you aren't quite sure what's causing that boxed-in feeling.

LARGE is when you can feel you're on the verge of breaking out. The box is pretty big, you're near the edge of its walls, and you're *almost* free. There isn't much left that's holding you back.

OUTSIDE THE BOX is when you're free and on the outside of the walls. No damn box at all, baby! You have wings and can go wherever you want without restrictions.

Now we realize that you might also look at one or more of these aspects of your life and say, "I don't have a clue." There's a big question mark over your head, and you're wandering around lost, thinking, *Am I in a box here? Hell if I know!* That's okay, too. It will become clearer as you turn each page and discover more about the expectations that may be keeping you from flying freely wherever the hell you want to go in life.

As you look at each box, you will see visually just how much breathing room you have or how restricted you are. We invite you to get messy and defy the expectations of a buttoned-up book owner. Go ahead and write all over the pages of this puppy. If you need permission, here it is.

We know this exercise might mean some uncomfortable truth-telling for you, but breaking out from what's holding you back has to start with the hard truth. (Be brave, remember?) For each of the boxes, trace a line around the outside walls if you feel your box is large, the middle walls if you feel your box is medium, or the inside walls if you feel your box is small. Or if you feel clueless about this one, circle the "clueless" option. If you're flying free outside the walls, congratulations! Circle the "flying free" option.

## Family of Origin Box

This box represents how you feel about your life with your parents, siblings, and extended family. Even if you're no longer in touch with anyone in your family—whether parents, siblings, aunts, uncles, or cousins—you're still emotionally affected by what happened in the household where you grew up. Are you stressed out or burned out in relation to your family? Do you feel your box is small, medium, or large, or do you feel free to express your true self with them? If you are no longer in touch with them, do you think what you experienced in your childhood home still has a significant hold on you?

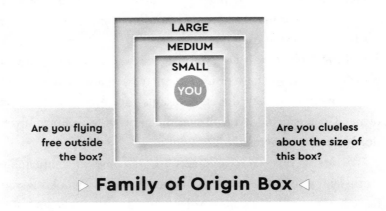

LARGE
MEDIUM
SMALL
YOU

Are you flying free outside the box?

Are you clueless about the size of this box?

▷ **Family of Origin Box** ◁

## Religion/Spirituality Box

This box is all about how boxed in you feel in your religious or spiritual life. Think carefully. Are you free and flying outside of the box, or are you stressed and restricted in this area of your life? Is your box small, medium, large, or open with no walls at all? For example, in Kelly's case, she felt restricted in a tiny box when she was young, but she has blown those walls wide open so that she's now free to be who she wants to be in her religious/spiritual life.

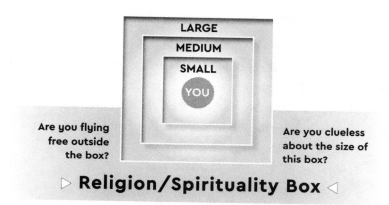

## ▷ Religion/Spirituality Box ◁

### Community Box

This box represents how satisfied you feel about your community and culture. Do you feel connected to the people in the area where you live, or do you feel suffocated by your community/culture? For example, maybe you feel you have to act a certain way to be accepted by the people in your community. How big is your box for this one?

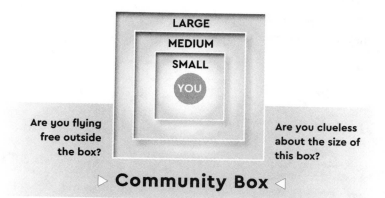

## ▷ Community Box ◁

## Love/Marriage/Kids Box

How satisfied do you feel right now about your love life or marriage/partnership? Bear in mind that this applies even if you aren't in a relationship. If you're very satisfied with your relationship or singlehood, you'll be free without a box at all. Otherwise, choose a small, medium, or large box based on how you feel in this area.

LARGE
MEDIUM
SMALL
YOU

Are you flying free outside the box?

Are you clueless about the size of this box?

▷ **Love/Marriage/Kids Box** ◁

## Career/Work Box

Do you enjoy your work, or is it a drudge? Do you love what you do, or do you wish you were doing something else? How you answer these questions will help you determine if your box in this area of your life is small, medium, large, or nonexistent.

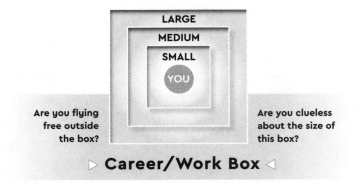

LARGE
MEDIUM
SMALL
YOU

Are you flying free outside the box?

Are you clueless about the size of this box?

▷ **Career/Work Box** ◁

## Gender Box

Do you feel that gender expectations in your life have put you in a box? This can mean expectations that make you act a certain way or hold you back from being yourself, whether you're male, female, nonbinary, or any gender expression. It might mean that you have experienced discrimination in your life. Do you feel your box in this area of your life is small, medium, large, or nonexistent?

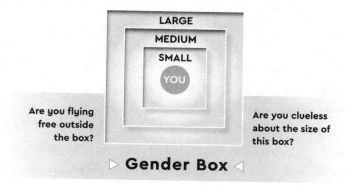

> Gender Box <

## Your Breaking Point: Slow Burn or Box on Fire?

If some of your boxes are small, medium, or large, you are in one of two situations: (1) a slow burn—feeling vaguely unsettled, maybe even frustrated for years, but not willing to do anything about it yet, or (2) with a box that's on fire as you sit in the center with the burning walls rapidly closing in on you. With number 2, there's no question you're fed up.

The truth of the matter is that we often refuse to take action until we reach that number-2 state. In change management, we call this the "burning platform." It's when the situation gets hot enough that we truly hate it. That's when we're willing to finally jump out of the box and change for the better. If you've picked up this book, chances are you have a burning platform in some area of your life—something that's eating at you and calling for change sooner rather than later.

But you don't have to wait for the walls of your boxes to catch fire. You can be in a medium or large box and still make changes if you figure out what you need in order to fly out from within those walls. And that's what we're prepared to help you do.

And no matter what you discovered in this exercise, don't judge yourself! We have all stuffed ourselves into boxes in life, and there's no shame in doing what you had to do to get where you are now. In this moment, you're revving up your bravery to make your life better. Give yourself a big gold star for that because not everybody's willing to fight for the life they want. *You are.*

*You'll notice that we haven't included some areas that are often included in these kinds of exercises, such as health/fitness and money/finances. We wanted to focus on the places where people we have interviewed tend to fall prey to expectations. But the BREAK process will work for these areas, too, if you'd like to try it at any time.*

—

Before you dive into the next part of the pre-change process, we want to make something else crystal clear: As you read these pages, don't you dare convince yourself that you're exempt from having the life you want. Don't tell yourself it's a pipe dream or that only some people get to fulfill their dreams. That's the worst kind of B.S. None of the people we know who have broken out and found freedom from expectations, including the two of us, have felt they had some kind of special sauce or magic to make it happen. They just did the work. And that's what it takes. The magic is all in your commitment to yourself.

The next chapters will help you unravel the expectations in different aspects of your life that have almost certainly resulted in any of the small boxes you've found yourself stuffed inside. Then, you'll know exactly where you need to break free in order to live the authentic life you're after. Take a deep breath, let your anticipation be your guide, and just be brave enough to turn the page.

# CHAPTER 2

# Okay, Freud, You Were Right about Our Parents

When we're kids, most of us don't think, "My family is so dysfunctional!" (At least maybe not until the teen years.) Instead, since we have no other experience to compare it to, we assume the way our family functions is the same as every other family.

Everything we learn from our parents is our foundation for how the world works.* Until we have some frame of reference from our friends' families or maybe a TV show, why would we think our family could or should be any different?

Early beliefs about life stick to us like the most adhesive glue you've ever seen (Krazy Glue times ten) and can put us in little boxes at a very young age. Think about how hard it is to get rid of

---

\* When we refer to "parents" in this chapter or elsewhere in the book, we mean the adults who served as your caregivers during your childhood. We realize that for you, this might have been grandparents, aunts, uncles, adopted parents, foster parents, or siblings. We'll use "parents" as a generic catch-all term.

the accent you learned when you were first taught to speak. The same is true, if not more so, of the family expectations.

Have you ever caught yourself acting like your mom or dad in a way you don't like? It's enough to make you want to crawl into a hole and hide. But this happens to all of us because we learned how to be people from watching them. That's why in this chapter, you will begin to unearth the expectations that your family held for you, both spoken and implied.

## THE FAMILY "RULE BOOK"

Every family has its own set of expectations and rules—again, some explicitly stated and others unspoken. Psychology calls this set of rules the "family system." It's how each individual family operates within itself and with the outside world.

Most of us come from a family system that had a mixture of both healthy and unhealthy rules and expectations. That can only make it harder to identify the ones that aren't doing us any favors. You might hear yourself say: "My parents clearly loved me, so what was wrong with them telling me what to do for a living?" Or: "My mom took such good care of me that she never let me out of her sight." But how have the rules and expectations underlying such statements actually affected you? That's what you have to figure out.

Sometimes, our parents expect too much of us, such as demanding we get all As in school, that we continue the family business, that we marry the kind of person they think we should, or that we never move too far away from them. Other times, they might expect too *little* of us, such as when they tell us we're incapable of doing anything worthwhile, that we're always going to be in trouble, or that we shouldn't try a difficult profession we love because we won't be successful. In both instances, the expectations impact the way we think about ourselves and what we believe we have permission to do in life.

These expectations often become beliefs that we carry as if they're hard truths. That's when we really get stuck in boxes! You might sincerely believe, maybe unconsciously, that you will never succeed. It takes awareness to uncover these beliefs, and it takes time to dismantle them.

Stop for a second and think about a negative belief you hold about yourself. Maybe you worry that you aren't smart enough or that other people don't like you. Do you know where that belief came from? There's a good chance it came from your parents, whether they said it outright or led you to believe it through their behavior and punishments.

Parents are also prone to say, "We know what's best for you." That's one of our personal "favorites" (sarcastic eye roll—even though Keri admits she says it to her son at times, just like most parents). Parental expectations are usually coming from a place of love, and when we're young, our parents often *do* know best. But now that we're grown-ass adults, we have to learn to step away from the assumption that what we were told as children still applies. Our parents are no longer the be-all and end-all of wisdom and authority.

The fact is that many parents see their children as a reflection of who *they* are. Sometimes, they want us to fulfill the dreams they never managed to make happen. Like the father who always wanted to go to college and now expects you to do so. Or the mother who wanted to break the glass ceiling in the corporate world and is living vicariously through you as you climb through the ranks.

As far as they are concerned, they are loving and parenting you in a healthy way. They may be doing what their parents did. Unless at some point someone stops to contemplate whether the expectations actually make sense. Even when parents try to do everything differently from their own parents, they can still inadvertently place unwanted expectations on their children.

Of course, there are wonderful expectations that parents contribute to our upbringing like being kind and helping others. For example, in Keri's family, all women worked. "We never talked about it," she says. "But seeing women kick butt from a young age meant I never questioned that I could have both a career and a family." It's up to each of us to determine which expectations are positive for us and which are negative.

Keri also wants to interject here that she *is*, after all, a parent herself, so she knows from experience that it's a crazy hard job. She tries not to inflict unwanted expectations on her son, but that doesn't mean she's successful 100 percent of the time. And if you're a parent, we aren't trying to make you feel lousy about yourself. All parents are human, and we're not trying to demonize anyone.

Still, the fact remains that at least by the time we reach adulthood, each of us is left with the task of living *our* one life based on our own true desires and expectations and nobody else's. And letting go of what our parents expect of us is no doubt one of the hardest things to do. Part of that job is seeing our parents objectively. It sucks, but it's necessary.

Many of us want so much to avoid that job that we continue to do what we did in childhood—we suppress our feelings and try our hardest to do what our parents want. In the process, we develop such a talent for pretending that we gradually lose track of our emotions, what we truly want, and ultimately, who we are as separate from our parents' image of us. It's like trying to see your nose by squeezing it right up against a mirror.

Then, one day, we suddenly realize that this person we became to please our parents (or perhaps prove them wrong) fits us about as good as a suit that's six sizes too small and missing a sleeve. It's too tight and ill-fitting for us to feel anything close to happy, but where did our own desires go? Where's our own identity? It got lost a long time ago while we were busy becoming *someone else* in an effort to please *everybody else*. Sigh.

Most of us aren't aware of all the requirements of becoming a person that we internalized from our parents at a young age. It isn't like they are all spelled out for us. We have to figure out a lot of them through observation alone.

Without awareness, we never get enough of a distance from the mirror to see the expectations we've accepted without question. Then, we might find ourselves unhappy in life with no idea why or how to make it better. That's why we harp on this self-awareness part so much! It's that important.

You might say, "Come on, Kelly and Keri, everybody's parents put expectations on them. That's just life!" Sure, that's true to some degree. But the research doesn't lie. It has been proven that parental expectations can have a long-term effect on us that isn't remotely pretty. In 2021, a study in Virginia of 184 people within a broad age range of thirteen to thirty-two found that the ones who had controlling parents were less independent and assertive, and they even struggled more in romantic relationships. Other studies have had similar results. There's no denying it: the more our parents impose their expectations on us, the more likely we'll have to work hard in adulthood to be autonomous and emotionally healthy.[1]

So, as you read this chapter, you might find some memories flooding back. We know that going straight into family stuff might feel like we're throwing you into the deep end of the pool. But it all starts in your family of origin. In a book about expectations, we've got to open that Pandora's box first. Examining your childhood is how you locate that kid you once were and heal the past so that you can discard what isn't working and grab hold of what will.

We realize that some of you may have experienced abuse, and you might need more support than we can offer as you recall what you went through in childhood. Please get that support if you need it! If you start to feel upset, take a deep breath, let out a big exhale, and take a break. Lean on somebody close to you when you need to vent or unload some sadness or grief. If you feel like crying—damn it, cry! It's good for you.

Remember that assessing your family history is a process. We'll give you an exercise at the end of the chapter to help you shed some light on it, but this isn't something you do in one fell swoop. While we will help get you started, you will need time. You may need a therapist to help you sort through the realizations that come, handle them emotionally, and untangle your own desires from the ones you were taught. In the meantime, please be patient with yourself every step of the way. Treat yourself with the kindness you would offer a child or close friend.

Now let's chat about some common family expectations. See if you recognize any of these in your family.

### WHO'S THE ASSHOLE?

There's a series on the social news aggregation website Reddit, in which people write in and ask, "Am I the

Asshole?" about disputes with family and friends. It's fascinating because it shows that our family systems and expectations are sometimes downright insane. In one story, a guy wrote that because he made more money than his sister, his whole family assumed he would automatically pay for her wedding—even though no one bothered to ask him how he felt about it. When he said no, everyone in his family turned on him.

Reddit users who read his story felt it was outrageous he was expected to foot the bill. Nevertheless, his family acted like this was the norm in society. This is a great example of a family system expectation that needed to be examined and confronted.

## EXPECTATION: DON'T AIR YOUR DIRTY LAUNDRY

This was a consistent message in Kelly's family. They felt they had to maintain the illusion for the outside world that there were no problems within the family. But they also didn't talk about problems behind their closed doors. It's one thing to pretend with outside people, but to have to pretend at home too? Sometimes, it seems to be the only way to make sure the adults feel comfortable.

"It was an unspoken rule, for example, that we didn't tell Dad he hurt our feelings because he wasn't going to apologize anyway," Kelly says. "Our family never had healthy discussions to resolve issues. If we had a disagreement, rather than discuss it or tell me he was sorry, my dad would just go days without saying a word to me. Sometimes he would perform an act of service, that is, he'd do something for me, so yes, while it was a nice gesture, it didn't address the actual issue. Since I couldn't talk about how I felt, I grew up rarely speaking up for myself."

Meanwhile, Kelly's mother handled that situation by becoming passive-aggressive. Since she felt she couldn't be direct, her negative feelings came out in indirect ways. She would mumble her frustrations to herself, even though everyone could still hear her. Yet, it was an unspoken rule that it was taboo to talk about it directly afterward.

"I don't know what the hell they thought they were hiding," Kelly says with a chuckle. "The unspoken message was that if you keep it all inside, it will just miraculously go away. But we all know that makes it worse. It just becomes a powder keg that eventually blows."

When we live with this expectation of repressing feelings, we learn to cope by becoming passive-aggressive, like Kelly's mother. Then, we expect others to figure out that we're upset and change their ways without a discussion, and so we end up sweeping important issues under the rug—all just to avoid talking about them openly. When our family teaches us to keep our mouth shut, it can show up at work and in our relationships as we avoid sticking up for ourselves and let problems fester until they become explosive.

## EXPECTATION: EVERYTHING IS FINE, AND YOUR EMOTIONS ARE NOT WELCOME HERE

When Keri was only about nine years old and visiting her father one weekend (about four years after her parents divorced), she was suddenly told that her dad and his girlfriend had gotten married. *What?* She was given no warning about it and wasn't even invited to the wedding. Instead, she stood there in shock as her father followed up his announcement with "Everything's fine."

Keri's first thought was, "This is anything but fine!"

But that phrase "everything's fine" was meant to shut down any emotions that might emerge. The message was: *Keep those emotions to yourself, little girl! We need to hold on to the illusion that you're happy with it.*

The marriage also meant she suddenly had two new stepbrothers, and her father insisted, "We're one big happy family." Ummm . . . nope! Keri didn't know this family at all, so she definitely didn't buy into the idea that they were a "big happy family." Yet, she felt she had to pretend everything was perfect. What she really felt was that she was unimportant—an afterthought.

Most people, including our parents, are not well equipped to manage the myriad of emotions we all feel—both their own and their children's. They might learn to deal with a baby's tears, but as soon as that baby is old enough to understand the word *no*, we're not only told what we can and can't *do*, but what we can and can't *feel*. And anger? Kids aren't allowed to express *that* in most households, but the adults can fight with one another and yell at the kids on a regular basis. Then there's the problem with tears after a certain age. Usually, girls are allowed, but as soon as boys reach age three or four, they might be told to "man up" if a tear dares to escape from their eyes.

When we can't talk about our feelings, we don't feel safe to be vulnerable, which means we don't feel safe being ourselves. "I felt forgotten when my father married into another family," Keri says, "and the expectation that I'd keep my feelings to myself stopped me from establishing an emotional bond with either of my parents because everything was on the surface. All communication between us was false." If you have to keep an illusion (i.e., denial) alive, how can you be truthful about how you feel?

For Keri, pretending everything was fine was also expected in her mother's home. "My mom had a case of extreme perfectionism. If anyone said in her presence that something was wrong, she took it to mean that *she* was imperfect. One day, after I was an adult, I said to her, 'I don't want to work for a corporation like you did.' She took my declaration so personally that she said, 'So you think I'm a bitch?' In her mind, if I didn't replicate her choices exactly in my own life, it not only meant *I* wasn't perfect, but it meant something was wrong with *her*. It rattled her fragile perfectionist image of herself. My life was a mirror for hers, and the reflection had to be perfect for her to feel okay."

The expectations of Keri's parents weren't explicitly stated, so she had to decode them based on her mother and father's behavior. In each household, she had to twist herself into the person they wanted until she ended up feeling like a pretzel. Have you ever felt twisted while trying to become what others want? A lot of people can identify with that experience.

Keri's issues at home spread into her relationships with friends. "I don't think I made the best friend because I didn't know how to be vulnerable," she says. "I was more competitive with other girls because that's what my mother was like. I didn't know how to be authentic. The kind of girl talk I saw in movies was foreign to me for such a long time, which is one of the reasons I cherish my friendship with Kelly so much."

Why would her parents find vulnerability and the truth so terrifying? If they were no longer allowed to deny everyone's feelings and pretend everything was fine, they might have to look at their choices and face up to their faults as parents. They would have to change. That's hardly a fun job. Naturally, we're all resistant to the truth when it hurts, but that old cliché about the truth setting you free is valid.

When we aren't allowed to bring our full range of emotions to the table, we hold back who we are and wear a mask to hide ourselves. Like Keri, we might struggle to be vulnerable, preventing our relationships from growing and becoming deeper. Then, if something painful happens to us, but we still pretend everything is fine, we might accept pain as inevitable as well as keep it to ourselves.

## EXPECTATION: MISTAKES ARE NOT ACCEPTABLE

"It's a joke in my family that my dad expects everyone to learn something easily," Kelly says. "He would show you how to do something once, and if you didn't immediately do it perfectly, he'd say, 'Move. I'll do it myself.' I'm sure he didn't mean for his impatience to communicate that mistakes weren't acceptable, but it did."

The effects of that message came to a head for her when she went away to college. She made it to the dorm, but before the first day of classes, she panicked and decided she wasn't going to be able to handle it. She was sure she would be a failure.

When she told her resident advisor at the dorms why she planned on leaving, he said, "I've never known anyone who failed at something before they even started." His comment helped her see that she could relax the impossible expectation she had internalized from her family. She stayed and was anything but a failure in college.

How many of us were expected to get all As in school or to be the best in a sport? How many of us were expected to always behave like a good little girl or boy, only to be punished when we fell short? The expectations might be stated outright or just implied when we're punished or recognize our parents' disappointment in us.

An unspoken expectation that mistakes are not acceptable can cause us to expect too much of ourselves. We might be afraid to try something new because we can't bear to fail during the learning process. We have to be willing to stumble before we get it right. Have you ever expected yourself to be an expert at something right out of the gate? Think about how silly that is. You can't captain a boat until you've learned "the ropes" on the crew. The only way to break out of a box is to risk making a mistake!

## BUCKING THE FAMILY SYSTEM

The family system is a powerful magnet. It will always want to bring us back to what's called *homeostasis*. That's a fancy psychological term for balance, except homeostasis in this case means the status quo because the *dysfunction* is what feels like balance to the people involved. Therefore, in this situation, homeostasis is unhealthy.

We humans tend to be afraid of the unknown, so we like to stick to the familiar—even if the familiar sucks. When one person goes against the rules, everybody else within the system feels like they're teetering on the edge of a cliff, ready to fall into the scary abyss of the unknown. This fear is unfounded, but that doesn't make it any less intense. Without a conscious understanding of the nature of their fear, they fight against the person who's diverging from the rules. Unless they have the awareness to say, "Sis is just following what's right for her, and that doesn't have to affect us or reflect on us," they might go into freak-out mode. The magnetic pull toward unhealthy homeostasis has taken hold because familiar equals safe.

When we break the rules of the family system, we violate something very personal to people, even if they don't know why. They believe those rules are not only the way it's supposed to be but the way it *has* to be.

Take Prince Harry from the royal family in England. Whether you love him or hate him, he's the contemporary poster child for bucking the family system and fucking expectations. In his memoir, *Spare*, he talks about some of the rigid expectations placed on him even when he was a child whose mother had just died in a horrible accident. For example, he was expected never to cry in public. He almost stopped himself from crying in private until he remembered no one was there to see him. He was also expected to walk behind his mother's coffin, despite the protests of some adults within the royal family, and appear before the grieving public no matter how uncomfortable he felt, all while suffering such an awful loss at the tender age of eleven.[2]

Obviously, he felt strongly that the box he was placed within was way too tight, so he stepped out of it in a way that caused big rifts in his family. First, he and his wife stepped back from their jobs as senior members of the British royal family. This was unheard-of and caused an enormous stir within the entire country. Then, he defied the expectation about not airing your dirty laundry by publishing his tell-all memoir, disclosing family information that most of them felt should remain private. Prince Harry chose what he felt was best for himself, his wife, and his children, choosing to speak his truth despite the repercussions. Again, whether you agree with him or not, it took a lot of courage to do what he did.

Most of us (thankfully) don't come from a family system that's centuries old and well-known by the whole world, but that doesn't mean our own family rules can't feel just as entrenched. And we often feel enormous guilt and shame about them, especially if the implication is that family comes first even if it means putting ourselves last and inflicting pain on ourselves in the process—similar to the case of the guy who was expected to pay for his sister's wedding. If we make a choice outside of the family's rulebook, they might cloak their disapproval in worry that we're going to be hurt, but frequently, what hurts us most is abiding by family rules that don't serve us.

Our podcast guest Natasha Bowman, author of *Crazy A.F.: How to Go from Being Burned Out, Unmotivated & Unhappy to Reclaiming Your Mental Health at Work!*, went through a lot when she broke an unspoken rule of her family's system. She's a powerhouse who impressed us immensely when we interviewed her. A modern-day pioneer of workplace equality, she inspires organizations to not just pay lip service to workplace rights, but to craft highly engaged cultures where every employee is truly dignified and valued for their contribution. She has also been an adjunct professor at Fordham University and is often referred to as the "workplace doctor."

No matter how successful we might be, however, it doesn't shield us from mental health challenges. Natasha struggled during the pandemic, but she hid it from everyone. "I would turn on my Zoom smile like everything was okay, but I wasn't okay," she told us. She had always met the expectation she'd set for herself that you wake up happy and grateful every day—with no allowance for bad days. (We're seeing the "Everything is fine, and your emotions are not welcome here" expectation at play.) But that was a heavy weight she couldn't maintain. Eventually, her mental health plummeted to such a degree that she attempted suicide. Several months later, after she had recovered, having received a diagnosis and proper treatment, she decided to share her story.

"I never saw myself trying to be a groundbreaker or advocate," she says. But she woke up one morning and felt compelled to post the following on social media: "This is the face of bipolar disorder" along with a description of what she had been going through. She received more than a hundred responses within a half hour. As the day progressed, her post had tens of thousands of likes and comments from all over the world, as people identified with her. "That's when I knew I made the right decision," she says. She practically stayed up all night so that she could answer every person.

Natasha says allowing herself to be that vulnerable and transparent online was a thoroughly positive experience . . . except for one thing. Her family couldn't handle it. Much like Kelly's family's expectation to not air dirty laundry, her parents and siblings felt so strongly that it was wrong of her to tell the public about something so private that they still refuse to speak to her. Obviously, they also had the expectation that the family comes first even though what Natasha most needed to do for herself was to speak her truth like Prince Harry did. Sometimes, the family system teaches us not to speak up for ourselves, and this silence can be the very thing that hurts us most.

Of course, her family's reaction has been tremendously painful for Natasha, but she says she has found a new chosen family among the people who have embraced her for her courage in telling the truth and helping others feel less alone.

Unfortunately, this is one of the risks we take when we decide to buck the family system and its expectations. A ten-year study based on the first national survey on family estrangement found that as many as 65 million Americans are or have been estranged from an immediate or extended family member, and some researchers believe estrangements are on the rise.[3]

Your first thought might be, "That's horrible!" And yes, it is. But let's look at it from another perspective. This statistic might also mean that more people are saying "fuck the expectations," refusing to be held hostage to the whims of anybody else, even their parents. They are refusing to be drawn back into unhealthy homeostasis. Sure, we'd all prefer if we could just get along and say, "live and let live," but if it's the difference between subjugating who we are and estrangement, it's worth the rift. It means that at least in some of these cases, people are standing up for themselves, and that's a good thing.

We don't want to scare you into thinking that refusing to follow your family rules will mean you will automatically lose your parents, siblings, or others. But it wouldn't be right if we didn't warn you that it's possible. Obviously, we have a strong bias toward flipping off unwanted expectations and doing what you need for yourself. But this is your life, and you get to decide what's worth the risk and what isn't. Sometimes, as long as family members don't out-and-out require that you abide by their rules, you can live the life of your choosing while maintaining connection. Few people are blessed with parents and siblings who don't get on their nerves at least some of the time, but it's up to you to decide which compromises you're prepared to make. You get to decide when you're comfortable keeping people in your life despite whatever differences of opinion you may have with them.

Our friend Adam had a falling-out with his family over his choice to be in a relationship with someone they didn't like. "My family members are all highly educated people," Adam says. "My mother has two degrees, and my stepfather has three. My sister became a lawyer, and my brother is a professor at a prestigious university. So, when I fell in love with a woman who never went to college, they were adamant that she wasn't right for me. 'We're not looking down on her, son, but she'll never be enough for you,' they told me. I guess they were just worried it wouldn't work out. Nevertheless, I didn't agree and wasn't going to break up with her because of their fears and prejudices." For almost two years, Adam barely spoke to his parents, brother, or sister. Then, when he started planning his wedding with his fiancée, Rita, he wondered if his family would even be willing to attend.

"It was terribly painful," he says, "and Rita felt awful. But it wasn't her fault. She's the most wonderful woman I've ever known, and I couldn't wait to spend the rest of my life with her. But I felt so sad that I might get married without my family there." So, Adam sat down and wrote a letter to all four of his immediate family members. He poured out his heart, telling them all the reasons why he had fallen in love with Rita and how much he wished they would get to know her better. He told them he really wanted them at his wedding and hoped they would be willing to heal the rift between them because he was getting married either way.

Luckily for Adam, his efforts worked. Both his parents and his siblings agreed to let go of their judgments of his fiancée and attend the wedding. Last time we heard, they have grown to love her as much as Adam does.

It's wonderful when people can find peace with their family despite defying expectations, and most of the time, it's worth making that effort. But if we acquiesce to their expectations and live a false life as a result, we never find peace. All we can do is try to help them see our point of view.

Both sets of our parents don't always agree with the choices we've made, but they no longer interfere with what we do. That may be true for you as well, yet it can still be difficult to break free from what you've always thought you were supposed to do and how you've always thought you were supposed to be. Again, discovering what you want can be a slow process, sort of like peeling an onion. For example, you might peel back one layer to reveal that you learned from your mother, through the behavior she modeled, to put your own desires aside and make other people's desires more important. Then, you might realize that a part of you resents this because you rarely even let yourself choose the movie or the restaurant when you go out with family or friends. That's the kind of thing you can quietly change as you begin to catch yourself putting your own wants aside. The next time you go out to dinner with friends, you can make a different choice and say, "I've always wanted to try the new Thai restaurant. What do you say we go there?"

Peeling the onion further might reveal that in childhood you were expected to take care of your brothers and sisters and make dinner for the whole family. As an adult, you might continue to take care of everyone at home, at work, and in your community, which has left you burned out and exhausted. In order to stop doing it all for everyone, you will have to learn to set boundaries and say no.

Speaking of boundaries, the kinds of expectations that cause real conflict in families are often a result of boundary violations, like the parent who shows up unannounced and expects you to drop everything, the sister who insists that you raise your kids her way, or the relative who expects you to tell them all your private business. In situations like that, standing up for yourself is usually necessary. While it might involve an uncomfortable conversation, the only resolution is to let the violator know that you need them to respect your boundaries. Sometimes, people push back, but if you're ready to nix expectations, you'll have to stand your ground and reiterate your boundaries as often as necessary.

## WERE YOU THE *WEIRD* ONE OR THE PERFECT ONE IN YOUR FAMILY?

Everyone in the family takes on a role within the family system. Sometimes, people get labeled based on these roles. For example, if we try to break the rules, we might get called *uncaring, stubborn, selfish, weird,* or *insert your own derogatory term.* Labeling the rule-breaker means the system can keep going without taking responsibility for the family's dysfunctional way of thinking.

If you were given a label or thrown into a role that didn't reflect who you are, know that they are not real or accurate. They don't mean anything, and none of us has to take them to heart. So, if you were called *the screw-up, the caretaker, the perfect one, the scaredy-cat, the weirdo,* or something else, here's a trash can: please drop it in there! Far too often, we absorb these labels as if they're a true description of who we are, and we allow them to diminish our self-esteem or make us try to live up to an image that puts undue pressure on us.

We believe our family is supposed to know us the best, so if they label us, we mistakenly think it has to be true. That can hurt like hell. If they use that label to describe us to people outside of the family, it can feel as if we've been branded with a scarlet letter. But this idea that our family knows us best is utter bullshit. In our experience, that couldn't be further from the truth—exactly because these roles are assigned to us in childhood, they usually have nothing to do with who we really are.

Has somebody else in your family already been labeled *weird*? This could be a brave rebel who has dared to buck the system before you, refusing to get pulled back into unhealthy homeostasis. For Kelly, this person was her grandmother, who was an inspirational badass. When her husband died, and she decided to live separately and unmarried from the man who was her companion, she stepped outside the system to become who she wanted to be and fucked everyone else's expectations in the process.

Of course, when we do buck the system and go against the family's rules, our parents and siblings may try to manipulate us back to their brand of homeostasis. They don't do this consciously, but it's their effort to maintain a feeling of safety. This is where that nasty magnetic pull comes in. But we can choose to fight to be true to ourselves like Kelly's grandmother did.

## STANDING UP FOR YOURSELF

If your family was like ours, conflict-averse, its members always pretending everything is fine, your tendency will be to do the same. But to assert yourself and move beyond expectations, you may have to speak up for yourself, like Adam did. For example, as adults, we shouldn't be expected to tell our parents everything about our personal life, show up at every family event, do everything they ask of us, listen to their opinions about *our* life, or accept unannounced visits.

Standing up for ourselves with our parents or even our siblings and extended family takes a lot of courage and can trigger us emotionally like nothing else. (There's that trusty magnetic pull back into unhealthy homeostasis again.) Kelly chose to write about her parents in this book, and that alone is violating the family rule of "don't air your dirty laundry." It wasn't easy, but it's the decision she made. "It's uncomfortable to think they might not be happy about it," she says, "but on the other hand, I'm good with me." Ultimately, we all have to reach that place in order to live according to what will make us happy and at peace with ourselves.

If you decide that you have to talk with a family member about a family rule, expectation, or boundary violation that needs to go the way of the dinosaur, you will need to prepare yourself for that conversation. We suggest practicing what you want to say so that you can hopefully avoid getting drawn into an argument. Practicing will also help you stay calm and not lose your cool, which would likely lead to a breakdown in communication. Think about times you might have had difficult conversations that were successful. What made those discussions work? What could you apply in this conversation to help manage the expectations of the other person involved? What support do you need to feel confident enough to have these conversations, and where can you get that support? Who could you practice with?

If you feel the conversation will inevitably turn into an argument, you might choose to write a letter or email like Adam. This allows you to think carefully about what you say, and it gives the other person time to think about their response.

Whatever you do, we have found it helps to maintain responsibility for your own feelings. Avoid placing blame on the other person, even if you feel blame is justified. In our experience, it also helps to be as truthful as you can about how you feel, keep the focus on you rather than what the other person has done "wrong," and stay as loving and kind as possible. It's the difference between saying, "You never let me know when you're stopping by" and "It would be helpful to me if you called ahead of time to make sure I'm free." Your parents or family members may act as though your honesty is a betrayal, but keep reminding yourself that the truth only betrays the denial (which, damn it, needs to be betrayed).

Phew! It's hard—we know. We don't recommend that you leap into having these encounters right away. Instead, it's best to finish reading the book before you gather your courage to talk about a difficult issue.

Then, don't be surprised if you set a boundary or defy an expectation, only to find that your parent or other family member ignores it or harps on it. To deal with their discomfort, they may become passive-aggressive or outright aggressive, desperately trying to stay in their version of homeostasis. It's difficult for people to change, so it becomes our responsibility to assert our boundaries and wishes repeatedly. Usually, we can find a way to stay both firm and kind while we do it.

But when another person, no matter who they are, refuses to respect your wishes for your own life, it's an unhealthy relationship. Of course, that doesn't mean you have to walk away from every unhealthy relationship in your life. If it's a parent, you might want to keep them around in spite of the issues you face with them. Only you can decide what you're willing to tolerate.

Here's an example of someone who chose to keep a difficult parent in her life. Our friend Mandy moved to New York from Kentucky when she was in her twenties, but her father never forgave her for it. He expected her to always stay close to his side. She sought her own life and didn't abide by that expectation, and so she endured his snide comments and guilt trips until the day he died. She chose not to cut him off despite his remarks, accepting that he was doing the best he could. "It would have been unacceptable," Mandy says, "if he had actually retaliated or prevented me from pursuing my great new life in New York, which by the way, is the best decision I ever made. My advice to people is to just be careful not to tolerate so much that they deny who they are and what they want. I think we truly enter adulthood when we stand up for ourselves and refuse to allow our parents to interfere with our lives."

Mandy's father expected her to adhere to the expectations that family always comes first and that children should respect their elders and bow to their wishes (even if it makes their adult child miserable). Those are rules in many families. How many of us were forced to do the bidding of adults even when it felt like a violation? When our parents said, "I'm just doing what's best for you," we were asked to trust them without reservations. As adults, we need to question if the perspectives of our elders were always correct and if their values align with ours. In other words, we're grown-ups now and must think for ourselves!

When you do get ready to stand up for yourself and speak out against an expectation, we recommend finding at least one person in your life who sees the true you. They will keep you anchored in your authenticity so that you don't get sucked back into dysfunctional homeostasis. Everybody's had the experience of going back to their childhood home and suddenly acting like they're thirteen years old again. So, you have to find a way to stay grounded in who you actually are, not who they want you to be. You have to know yourself as separate from the system, and the best way we know to get to know that real version of you is in therapy. At least that's what worked for us.

In psychology, they say that just asking questions changes the game. So that's what we're going to do next—ask you some key questions to begin the process of uncovering the unwanted expectations of your family so you can break free of that particular box.

## Ask Yourself: Parental Expectations

Let's look at the family expectations that may be causing you to feel stuck. Some of the stories in the chapter may have sparked some insights for you.

Think about the expectations that your family may have placed on you throughout your life and write down what comes to mind.

If you find yourself struggling with this, look back at the box you created in chapter 1 for your family of origin. How boxed in do you feel with your family—small, medium, large, or free-flying on the outside? This will tell you a great deal about how much you might still be living by family expectations.

Then, look at the other boxes. In what areas of your life are you currently dissatisfied? Does your life look like your parents' life in any of these areas? If so, ask yourself, and be as honest as you can: Are you behaving in this area of your life as you were expected to by your family? If so, are you happy about that choice, or have you ever thought about diverging from those expectations?

If you take a moment to entertain the possibility of doing something different, how does it feel? If it immediately feels scary, ask yourself what's scary about it. Do you worry that your family would object or judge? If they did object or judge, what's the worst-case scenario that you can imagine? Is that worst-case likely or unlikely? Most of the time, we catastrophize and worry about scenarios that would probably never happen.

If you did do that something different, how would it feel if you weren't afraid of your family's reaction? Can you imagine it? Would you feel much more freedom to change if the fear wasn't there?

Write down your thoughts, but don't rush to finish this. It will take some soul-searching, and you may need to come back to this exercise later. Again, you might want to talk to a therapist, close friend, or sibling about what comes to mind. As long as they have no personal agenda, an outsider's perspective can provide helpful insights.

When you feel you have unearthed some of the parental or family expectations that have held you back, write down the one that you feel has been the most influential and consequential in your life. Which one is boxing you in the most, whether your parents are still requiring it of you or you're now simply requiring it of yourself because you learned it in childhood?

Here are some examples of what someone might write:

*My family still expects me to drop everything and neglect my own kids when any of them has a crisis.*

*My grandparents, who raised me, expected me to always be a "good girl" and never speak up for myself. As a result, even though my grandparents are no longer with us, I have allowed people to treat me poorly my whole life.*

*My father expected me, and still expects me, to always fail. Therefore, I expect myself to always fail, and it's almost always a self-fulfilling prophecy. Most of the time, I just don't try anymore because I assume I can't possibly succeed.*

Now it's your turn. What is the most influential expectation for you? Make some notes about your new insights and how you feel about them.

Please hold on to what you write in all of the exercises because you will refer to your notes later.

# CHAPTER 3
# OMG. Yep, Those Religious Expectations

If you think family rules are hard to break, try religion and spirituality! Many of us question our parents or talk about them in therapy, but questioning religion? That's the minefield of all minefields (even worse than politics). Let's face it: parents may mess up their children, but the damage is nothing like the scale of the Spanish Inquisition.

While working on this chapter, we were floored to find out that there are more than 4,000 religions in the world! (We're still shocked.) But many of us have walked away from the religion of our parents or the communities we grew up in.** Less than 50 percent of the US population now belongs to a religious congregation, and more than a billion people worldwide self-identify as nonreligious or atheist.[1]

---

** While our personal experiences are Christian or agnostic, religion in this chapter refers to any religion.

Even if we leave, our family or community might maintain spiritual expectations of us that can cause problems. And some of the residual expectations of religion can linger in our psyche. Like family expectations, they make Krazy Glue seem like water.

Even those who adopt a more new-age spiritual approach to life can be saddled with expectations. *Manifest abundance! Don't you dare entertain a negative thought! Ommmmm . . .* We might even leave a religion to get out of a box with very tight walls, only to find ourselves stuck in a brand-new box with walls just as tight. Spiritual expectations can cause us to feel like we don't belong, like we aren't good enough, or like we aren't safe to express our true selves. All of this can make for a scalding-hot psychological soup. (Be careful not to burn yourself!)

Let's unravel some of the common expectations that might still be lingering whether you adhere to a particular religion, consider yourself spiritual but not religious, or even if you aren't religious at all.

## EXPECTATION: YOU'VE GOTTA BE PERFECT TO GO TO HEAVEN

Kelly was raised in the Catholic Church, but she has turned her back on it. "The belief system included the idea that if you didn't get baptized, you wouldn't go to heaven," she says.

This supposed standard for entry into heaven was hard for her to swallow. "The concept that babies are born with original sin is hard to stomach," Kelly says. "Apparently, the earlier you baptize your child, the better off they'll be because, what if they happen to die before the priest pours the so-called holy water on them?" The message is that we're inherently flawed, and that even as babies, we are somehow sinners.

Kelly remembers receiving the sacrament of Penance, when she was about eight years old. That's when she and the other third-graders first had to confess their sins to a priest. Some of her friends took the sacrament so seriously that they stepped out of the confessional in tears. "Do we need an intermediary for confession? I don't know about you, but I prefer my direct relationship with God," she says.

It isn't as if Kelly or the other kids had any great sins to report. Seriously, what kinds of sins did you commit as a child? Disobeying your parents by sneaking your peas into the trash instead of eating them? Saying an occasional curse word? In other words, pretty normal things that every child does. Why are these considered sins?

Even for people who aren't religious and didn't grow up in any particular religion, modern Western society is rooted in Judeo-Christian beliefs. So, we may unconsciously carry the weight of these high standards in our unconscious mind and feel guilty when we inevitably miss the mark.

In the Old Testament, the word for sin is *khata*, which means to "miss the goal." Who hasn't done that? Our self-worth can take a major hit as we try to measure up without an ounce of allowance for being human. Many of us have a tendency to label ourselves as *bad* when we make mistakes, and some of us might even become weighed down by self-hatred.

Our friend Maya grew up in an evangelical Christian household and felt like she was a bad person if she got angry even for a moment. "I felt like I had to ask forgiveness from Jesus for every little thing or it meant I would go to hell," she says. "The message was that if you sin and then die before you've had a chance to ask for forgiveness, you'll burn forever. Yet, the next message was that God loves us. Eventually, I realized those were contradictory, but it took me a long time to get over thinking I was a bad person for not being perfect 24/7."

Marcia Anglarill, a public diplomacy officer with the U.S. Department of State, had a similar experience growing up in her Catholic household. As a result, she suffered a great deal from religious guilt. The teachings of her religion were very much embedded in her during her childhood. "I even went through a confirmation process," she says. But a seed was planted in eighth grade when a secular teacher taught evolution in her school, which was probably against the rules. For the first time, she began to wonder if all she had been taught was the truth.

Still, it wasn't until she went to university that conversations with others began to open her eyes to truly consider different ways of thinking. In her courses, she was actively encouraged to question everything. Before long, she realized she no longer believed in what she'd been taught by her church, particularly how it often instilled intense guilt in followers for the slightest mistakes. "Guilt holds you back in your life," she says, "and makes you think twice about taking risks." Like Maya, Marcia judged herself harshly when she was young and felt she constantly had to run to confession. Afraid to fall short of her religion's standards, she felt squeezed into a tiny box that kept her from living her life fully.

It took her a long time to be able to let go of that guilt, but her self-esteem gradually improved, and she was able to be more forgiving of her mistakes. In that way, her box expanded until she had plenty of breathing room and eventually left it entirely.

Nevertheless, she values the essence of religion and even the Catholicism that led to her guilty feelings, and she acknowledges that not all Catholic or Christian churches instill the kind of guilt she experienced. "There are obviously good things about having faith," she says. "But there are too many ways in which religion is controlling, and it closes your mind to other views and ideas. And I find this whole idea that any religion is the only one to be problematic."

Her mother was devastated at first that Marcia turned her back on Catholicism, but eventually, her mom came to accept it, at least to a large degree. Today, Marcia considers herself a spiritual person who doesn't identify with any religious institution, and she says this works much better for her because she is now much easier on herself and feels freer to step out of the box and take risks. If she makes a mistake, she now knows it's just because she's human.

The reality is that we all get jealous, feel petty, swear from time to time, overreact, lash out, and do stupid shit. It's what humans do. Each of us has to learn how to stop judging ourselves and constantly looking for what's wrong with us.

The best way we know for you to do that is to begin to catch yourself in the act of judgment. If you become more aware of when you put yourself down or get on your own case for a mistake, you can consciously stop yourself, as Marcia has learned to do, and say, "No, it's okay to be a human being. I can strive to do better without beating myself up over it. I'm not a bad person because I'm imperfect."

## EXPECTATION: YOU MUST ADHERE TO ALL OF OUR BELIEFS TO BE IN THE CLUB

Religion or even spiritual groups can be like a membership. When we join a club, whether it's a church, a moon circle, a coven of witches, or a cult, we are often told outright (or at least it's strongly implied) that we must accept all the beliefs of the group to be a member. It's a pledge of allegiance to the group-think mentality.

We humans are hardwired to want to belong, and the expectation is that to belong we have to speak the language and follow all the rules. It's usually at least implied that we will be shunned and isolated if we don't follow the group-think 100 percent.

In the 1970s, a psychologist named Henri Tajfel wanted to know just how prone we are to go along with the pack and favor the members of our own group (the so-called in-group) over a different group (the so-called out-group). His research team gathered teenage boys and showed them slides of paintings by two artists. The researchers told the boys they would be divided into two groups based on which painter they liked best, but they were actually divided up randomly. The boys were then asked to give awards to other members of both groups. They were given a list of all the boys, each identified by their group and an individual ID number. When giving out the awards, the boys favored members of their own group—the other boys they believed preferred the same painter. They did this even though they had never met the other boys and had no way of knowing if there was anything to gain from it.[2] But wait, aren't teenagers particularly prone to that kind of behavior? Sure, but those experiments have been replicated many times with adults. In other words, we don't tend to outgrow this one that much.

Some religious groups even expect their members to hate others who think differently, targeting that hatred at other religious groups or at those who identify as LGBTQIA+. The effects of religious bigotry on the LGBTQIA+ community are especially disturbing since attacks against them are on the rise.[3] This is when group-think becomes dangerous.

Going along with a group gets extreme in cults, for example, in cases like NXIVM, whose members were expected to brand their skin with the cult leader's initials. Blech!

Even in the most loving of religious or spiritual groups, it might be frowned upon to question any of the beliefs. "If a church member questioned anything in my Catholic church," Kelly says, "they were told that what was being taught was the way to enlightenment. If any of us didn't believe it, it was our problem, and we were treated to the cliché, 'God works in mysterious ways.' That was a blanket cop-out statement used to shut everyone up. If we questioned clergy, we were told we were questioning God, and He was up on his throne really mad about it."

So, if you think your family had an iron hold on you, religion can be far stronger. After all, if you defy expectations of the latter, you might be told you'll go to hell or be reincarnated as a cockroach!

It's natural to worry what would happen if we said no to a group we want to belong to, but we all have the right to make our own choices. We can reject the expectation that to be a part of a group, we have to hate another group. We have to ask ourselves: *Do I really want to be part of a group that hates or is intolerant?* And we have to ask ourselves if we can remain part of a group while quietly rejecting some of its beliefs. That can certainly work in many cases, but not if a group is too pushy about its rules. In that case, we might need to look for a new group that's more in line with our personal values.

## EXPECTATION: ARE YOUR CRYSTALS IN ORDER?— SPIRITUALITY HAS TO LOOK A CERTAIN WAY

What does it mean to be spiritual? Ask two different people, and you'll get two different answers. Yet, when we join a group, formally or informally, it will have very specific ideas about what it means to be spiritual. And we're expected to be spiritual in the same way.

Even in groups that seem to be all about personal freedom, we might still be expected to eat a vegan diet, go to yoga class, meditate daily, and wear flowy clothes with our fingers firmly in the mudra position. In other words, it isn't just organized religion that places expectations on us.

Someone's brand of spirituality might entail writing affirmations and avoiding negativity at all costs. It can be its own kind of perfectionism that stuffs them in a little box already so crowded with crystals that they can't even fit a yoga breath in edgewise. So if the spirituality you've adopted isn't actually working for you, it's your prerogative to change it to what you need.

Our podcast guest Maggie Malone changed her religion. She is an Olympian—the first female javelin thrower to win an NCAA title and US Olympic Team Trials title in the same season.

Maggie was raised Catholic, but she says she was unable to understand God's love and grace, "specifically the grace of Jesus," until she found a nondenominational church that was right for her. "I wanted to know who God is," she says. "Becoming a part of this new church community absolutely has changed my life forever. I definitely came to a really low point after the Olympics. They call it the 'Olympic hangover.' And I felt it 100 percent. I didn't realize a lot of other Olympic athletes had felt that. I felt so alone. I wasn't performing well. I was injured . . . The thing that gave me the most joy at the time now became the biggest source of pain in my life."

The "Olympic hangover" affects many athletes who reach the pinnacle of success at a young age but then have to go back to everyday life. Only a handful of Olympic athletes receive big endorsement deals, so many face financial problems after competing or even winning a medal.

Friends connected Maggie with a Christian counselor who helped her with the issues she was facing. "She asked hard questions that I was used to skirting around most of my life, and she would not let me skirt them," Maggie says. The counselor helped her make sense of her life from a realistic perspective post-Olympics and she began to recover from the hangover. Maggie has been able to continue to compete and has qualified for the next Olympics. But now she knows what to expect and has her faith as a strong foundation.

## EXPECTATION: BUT YOU *MUST* HAVE A RELIGION!

It may seem like we are trashing religion in this chapter, but we promise we're only trashing the bad stuff. Religious and spiritual groups do a lot of good in the world and provide comfort and community to millions, just as Maggie experienced. We're totally on board with that!

But what happens if you aren't religious at all and maybe not even spiritual? You might feel like an oddball or entirely left out of the conversation.

You've heard a lot in this chapter about Kelly's background in Catholicism, but what about Keri's religious or spiritual background?

Well, Keri's family wasn't religious at all, and she grew up not believing in anything in particular. When classmates asked her to name her religion, she'd say, "I'm a person."

But the conversation didn't end there. Her friends had more questions.

"No, what *religion* are you?" they'd push.

"I'm not anything."

Inevitably, they would gasp in response and say, "You can't mean that! Well then, we'll pray for you."

She found that many people expect everyone to follow some brand of religion or spiritual program, and if someone doesn't, the assumption is that something's wrong with them. "People have no problem telling me I'll go to hell," she says. *"Can't I just be a person?!"*

Yes, we think it's quite all right to just be a person with no religious affiliation. Agnostics and atheists deserve more than just free time on Sundays. Nobody owes anyone else an explanation for how they choose to live.

The two of us feel strongly that it's important to respect all beliefs, and we advocate for everyone's right to believe and practice as they wish—as long as they don't harm anyone else or force their beliefs onto others. Besides, underneath it all, every single one of us is just a person!

We hope we've given you some thoughts to chew on in this chapter, so let's look at where expectations having to do with religion or spirituality (or the lack thereof) might have placed you in a small, medium, or large box in life. How much are you squeezed?

## Ask Yourself: Religious, Spiritual, or Atheist Expectations?

As you did in the last chapter, begin to think about the expectations that you feel in your religious or spiritual life, even if you have no religion or spirituality, per se. First, take a look at the religion box you created at the end of chapter 1. What size is it? Do you need to adjust the size now that you have read this chapter?

Make a list of any unwanted religious or spiritual expectations that you feel you must meet. Have any of these expectations been outright damaging to you? If so, make note of what has been harmful about them.

What do you feel are the consequences of continuing to meet these expectations for the rest of your life? What within yourself would you have to sacrifice, and is that sacrifice worth it? Only you can decide, but it's important to think about what you are giving up if you choose to continue versus if you choose to stop.

Which expectation has been the most influential and consequential in your life? Which one is boxing you in the most, whether you're still practicing the religion or you're now simply requiring it of yourself because you learned it in childhood? Is this unwanted expectation keeping your box smaller and more suffocating than it has to be?

If you let go of the most consequential expectation you listed, how would your box get bigger and gain more breathing room, or could you fly out of the box entirely? Would you have to leave your religion or spiritual group, or could you quietly let go of this expectation and stay within the group?

If you did choose to stop meeting this expectation, how would your life look? What would be different?

Last, ask yourself: How do you want your spiritual/religious life to look going forward? What needs to change in order to achieve that goal, and what support do you need to make it happen? For example, do you feel you want more spirituality in your life or less?

Write down your thoughts, but just like the family issues, don't rush to finish this. It will also take some soul-searching, and you may need to come back to this exercise later. Again, you might want to talk to a therapist or close friend. If you're seriously considering leaving your religion entirely, it might be helpful to find someone who has already done it. They would probably have some insight to help you make this difficult decision.

# CHAPTER 4
# Boys Will Be Boys, But Just Be a Good Girl

"Are you familiar with what a bank is? You see, you go in and deposit or withdraw money . . ." This is what a high-level executive said to us—two fully grown women—when we were tasked with interviewing him for a client. He honestly thought women who own their own consulting firm were unfamiliar with the basic concept of a bank. (We still can't believe this happened.) Sometimes, people don't expect too much of us. Instead, they expect us to be stupid, and unfortunately, this often happens due to our gender.

So this chapter is about those dreaded gender expectations, but not just the ones placed on women. We're going to cover the gamut before this chapter is over. No one gets by in our society without facing gender expectations, and the boxes they put us into are usually pretty damn small!

First, however, since we *are* women after all, we'll talk about some of our own experiences of sexism.

We are often called the "HR girls" or "training girls." (Is it likely men would ever be called the "HR boys"? We don't think so.) An executive once actually patted Keri's shoulder and said, "Here's my training girl."

She already had her PhD, so she quickly snapped back, "No, I'm your doctor of talent!" (How's that for "resetting" someone's expectation?)

Another time, when Keri still worked for a corporation, she was in a meeting where her male direct report was repeatedly treated like *he* was the manager. "He was uncomfortable with it and kept referring to me as *his* manager," Keri says. "But still, the other guys in the room didn't get it." That might occasionally happen with two men if, say, the male direct report is older than the male manager, but otherwise, it's most common when a woman is in the managerial position. Have you ever been in a situation where people automatically assumed the man in the room was the person of authority, or have you caught yourself making that assumption? This is one of the many ways unwanted or unconscious gender biases can creep up on us.

As women, we frequently start in a one-down position, or somebody tries to put us there. When Kelly was already in her mid-thirties, her company hired an outside male consultant to conduct a sales training with its leaders. After she presented the results of an exercise they'd been given, the consultant said, "Good job, little lady!" (Couldn't you just gag?) Even the other men in the room were shocked. She chose in the moment not to say anything to the consultant, but she let his female colleague know through nonverbal communication that it was inappropriate. Later, the colleague approached Kelly and apologized, agreeing it was an unacceptable comment. Kelly said, "Well, he's the one who's supposed to address it, isn't he, not you?"

Even when we achieve something great, there is often a man or two (or ten) ready to diminish it. When Keri was at university, she received some accolades from a professor while researching hostage negotiation with him, and he nominated her for an award. When the guy she was dating found out, he asked her, "Does the professor like you? Are you sleeping with him?" That could have been his insecurity talking, but the implication was still that it couldn't possibly be due to her academic abilities. (We'll bet you can guess how long the relationship with that guy lasted. If you said ten seconds, you'd be about right.)

Take a moment and reflect on some of the gender expectations you may have faced in your own life. What have people expected from you because you are female, male, transgender, or gender nonconforming? What have you expected from yourself as it relates to your gender identity? It can be very eye-opening to consider. If you're a man, you might not have thought about this at all, but there are plenty of expectations placed on men as well. We'll explore some of those below.

## EXPECTATION: BE A GOOD GIRL

When you notice someone putting a gender expectation on you, it might feel difficult to speak up. Both of us have struggled with when and how often to point these out. The reality is that we can't take a swing at everyone because it happens so frequently that it would become our sole profession (and last time we checked, that job pays a big fat zero). Plus, as women, if we get upset, we're usually labeled as a *bitch, too emotional, too sensitive,* someone with an *attitude problem,* or someone who's *not a team player.* In other words, "boys will be boys, so won't you just be a good little girl and shut up about it?" Those are the kinds of expectations we're talking about.

That doesn't mean we always stay quiet—not by a long shot. To do that would be to lie down and play dead, never letting someone know they were ignorant at best or way out of line at worst. But it's true that we all have to pick our battles. Any group that suffers from regular bias or prejudice has had to deal with this because there just isn't enough time or energy in the universe to fight every bigot we encounter.

Still, the societal expectation that women get too emotional follows us around like a shadow. But guess what? It's total B.S., and we have the research to prove it. A study in 2021 followed 142 men and women for seventy-five days and found that men's and women's emotions fluctuate with *no discernable differences.* The study's senior author, Adriene Beltz, an assistant professor of psychology, said, "A man whose emotions fluctuate during a sporting event is described as 'passionate.' But a woman whose emotions change due to any event, even if strongly provoked, is considered 'irrational.'"[1]

As assertive as both of us have become, we know that being female means we have to stay mindful of how our directness can come across to someone who has bought into this false belief about women's emotions. We wouldn't have to worry about this if we were men, but sometimes, we just want to do business and not have to deal with wrongheaded perceptions. We can be very straightforward, but we admit that we do smile more often to soften our presentation, and we strive to stay calm rather than get upset. It's even worse for Black women, who are often automatically perceived as aggressive when they speak their minds. All of this is 100 percent unfair, but it's something we have to be aware of in order to get through the day without someone projecting their biases on us (or without losing our shit).

## GENDER EXPECTATIONS SCREW MEN UP, TOO

Societal norms encourage boys to suppress almost all emotions except for anger, so they're likely to develop a false self to hide their shame about their supposedly unacceptable feelings. This means they may be less likely to be authentic, less self-aware, and less likely to admit they need help compared to girls. (It turns out the joke about men being too stubborn to ask for directions has a real basis in psychology.)

A 2018 article in *Psychology Today* put it this way: "The threat to men who have accepted a narrow definition of what it means to be a man is very real. Self-harm, depression, anxiety, and aggressive attacks on others may be the consequence of having to hold in any thought or feeling that could expose a man to ridicule or judgment."[2]

There has been a lot of talk about "toxic masculinity" and how it is responsible for violence against women, and that's true. But it's also killing men and boys—literally. The proof is in the heartbreak: men and boys commit 80 percent of the suicides in the US even though they only make up 50 percent of the population.[3]

A friend's son, Peter, freely admits that he got involved with drugs in his teens because he didn't know how to express his emotions. "All of the men in my family, including my dad, were super stoic," he says. "They only talked about sports, never hugged, and never expressed the slightest vulnerability or affection in front of each other. The only time my father's façade cracked a little was when he kissed my mother. The unspoken expectation was that men had to be strong and that if you showed emotions, you weren't masculine enough. My friends at school weren't much better. If anybody got hurt during football practice and cried, they caught hell for it from all the other guys."

When he turned sixteen and his girlfriend's family moved away, Peter lost his only support for coping with his pain. So he turned to marijuana and later heroin. To finance his habit, he started selling and ended up incarcerated.

"Rehab was like a new life for me," Peter says. "For the first time, I saw men telling the truth about what they felt. It was such a relief to be able to say it out loud. It wasn't easy at first, but since everybody was patient with me while I learned to identify and express my feelings, I started to get a handle on them. Now, I live for therapy. I love being able to tell people how I feel and no longer equate stoicism with masculinity. It's been like a whole new life."

The point is that we have a lot of gender expectations in our society that diminish the fullness of who we are. Men don't have to be invulnerable and unemotional in order to be masculine, and women don't have to be quiet and constantly accommodating in order to be feminine. These restrictions prevent us from being true to who we are and expressing all of who we are. Yet, these are exactly the kinds of gender expectations that continue to keep us in suffocating boxes if we let them.

Stop for a moment and think about how gender expectations of men and boys have had an impact on your life. If you're male, we suspect the impact has been huge because you may have felt, like Peter, that you couldn't express any feelings of vulnerability without someone making fun of you. And like him, you might benefit from therapy.

# EXPECTATION: I HAVE TO
# BE THE BREADWINNER

For some men, there is the added weight of believing they have to be the family's breadwinner. Commonly, men are valued based on how much *bacon* (i.e., money) they can bring home, which keeps them working hard and sometimes excessively long hours. Our podcast guest Tom Nehila fell into that trap but didn't become aware of it until he suffered some big losses. Tom is a chief financial officer (CFO) and a volunteer board member for the Embrace Kids Foundation, which serves families of children with serious health challenges.

"I believed that my role in life was to provide for the family," Tom told us. He thought he had to work as hard as necessary, whether it meant commuting for an hour and a half or flying across the country. "I let work become too much of who I was," he says. His marriage fell apart, and he readily admits that his priorities were screwed up. "I wasn't there to listen to the challenges and issues she [his wife] was dealing with on a daily basis," he says. "That's probably the biggest cause of what separated us . . . I viewed my role as to go to work, make money, and allow the family to live, to grow, and to prosper in one sense—but not in the truest sense of the word, which means the family being interconnected with one another." His advice to men is that a marriage is a partnership that requires deep listening and being there for one another. "Take care of your friends," he stresses. "Take care of your family. Life is too damn short."

Despite the pressure that many men put on themselves to be the breadwinner, it turns out to be yet another outmoded gender expectation. Men are the breadwinners in just 55 percent of US marriages, which is much lower than in previous generations. Regardless, society doesn't make it easy for men to turn their back on this expectation. Waiters still tend to hand the check to the man at the table, both men and women might chuckle about a stay-at-home dad as if they're a joke, and men's restrooms often don't include changing tables, making it hard for men to go out with their infants unless a female comes along.

Keri's husband, Steve, believes men need to learn to see their worth beyond making money. An artist and teacher, Steve was the primary caregiver for their son when he was younger, while Keri was the primary moneymaker. He grew up in a household where both parents worked. "I was a latchkey kid," he says. "I didn't have a stay-at-home mom like June Cleaver from the old *Leave It to Beaver* TV show. And I've always been an artist and been good at it. To not be an artist would be to give up on something I always considered a gift."

While Steve has certainly heard the rumblings from others who think it's wrong or weird for a man to be the primary parent rather than primary breadwinner, he hasn't let it bother him. He understands the psychological underpinnings of those limiting societal expectations, and he isn't interested in falling prey to them.

Of course, we know it's easier said than done for many men to get past societal conditioning and see their worth beyond money. But we're nothing if not relentless, so we'll say it again: awareness is everything, and therapy is priceless! Meanwhile, as women, we can also stop perpetuating this gender trope, showing men they're worth so much more than the contents of their wallet and that they don't have to live up to a tired (yawn) rule.

## A WOMAN'S PLACE IS . . . IN BUSINESS

The World Economic Forum has already proven that when more women are in the workforce, productivity increases, which means everyone's salaries increase, including men's.[4] So why don't we as a society make more of an effort to advance women in business?

If you answered "childcare," you'd be right, at least in part. (We'll pause while you scream into a pillow.)

Unfortunately for women, we are still the ones who pull more of the weight in terms of housework and childcare.[5] That's a gender expectation that isn't changing nearly fast enough. In other words, change some diapers and pick up the vacuum, boys! With women still performing most of the unpaid domestic labor, we need to talk next about gender expectations in the workplace and the overall economy.

When Keri first joined the workforce, she didn't know many women at her company or in her community who had children and were also at the C-suite level. Either they were single or their children were already grown. This, of course, was not true of the men, who were almost expected to have young children at home. "When I had a baby," Keri says, "I was very clear that I wanted people to know that I was a mother. I wanted them to see that I still had a position of authority plus a baby."

One night after her son had been born, while she was working late, a male colleague saw her and said, "You should go home to be with your family!" But what about *his* family? Sadly, another woman might just as easily have said this to her . . . but probably not to a male colleague.

Our podcast guest novelist Liz Alterman told us about the time her husband was out of work. People automatically asked her for his résumé to try to help him find a new job. But when she was the one out of work, the common remark was, "How nice that you'll now have more time with your kids!" It was disheartening for her to find out how much less a woman's contributions in the workplace were valued.

Why shouldn't we expect a man to also go home to spend time with his family? Why should we think it isn't right for a woman to work late because her family supposedly needs her more than the man in the household? Again, this is why we bang the drum on awareness so much. Until we stop to think about these expectations that have been ingrained in us from a young age, either from family or society, we don't even know they are there. We don't even realize we might be stuffing ourselves (or someone else) in a box.

When we worked in Human Resources in the corporate world, we spent a lot of time listening to executives discuss candidates behind closed doors. Once, during succession planning, when a woman had become pregnant, one of the men said, "We don't know if she's going to come back," and the others nodded in agreement. When they started discussing a male candidate who had just had twins, Keri said, "Oh, I don't know if he'll come back." Everyone in the room looked at her like she had eels coming out of her ears. Her point didn't even penetrate their brains. They moved on without acknowledging her comment. That's how unconsciously accepting we are about these expectations.

Yet, a 2023 article in *Fast Company* titled "Why Offering Paid Maternity Leave Is Good for Business" provides considerable evidence that it would cost us less to provide childcare at work and increase family leave than it costs to replace employees.[6] As a society, we're so stuck in our biases and expectations that we continue to ignore the data that's as clear as the noses on our faces. A 2023 article in *Ms.* magazine called "Dads Get Paid More When They Have Kids—as Moms Earn Less," described the phenomenon called the "parenthood paradox," in which women make less money after they have children, while men make more. The phenomenon where fathers get more hours and a bonus has its own name—the "fatherhood wage premium"—while what women experience when they become mothers is called the "motherhood penalty." It's worse still for women of color than for white women (no surprise).

What can we do? Well, obviously, the fixes aren't easy, but we can each fight against these gender expectations in our own world when possible and enter the voting booth with these issues in mind.

## EXPECTATION: BE PASSIVE AND AGGRESSIVE

*Gah!* What's a woman to do when we're supposed to be quiet, sweet, *and* forceful? At our friend Carla's video game company, a man received a promotion that she thought she would get, even though he had four years less experience. "I had won awards in my field," Carla says. "I couldn't understand why I was passed over for someone less qualified than me. A good friend in management confided in me that I wasn't chosen because they saw me as 'not forceful enough.' It seemed to me that I was penalized for being feminine. I even spoke to lawyers about filing a discrimination lawsuit, but they felt it would be a hard one to win. So I started looking for a better job, and I found one at a company that valued my managerial style. I'm able to get my team to perform very well through valuing their contributions and praising them rather than being 'forceful' in a stereotypically masculine way. Ultimately, it turned out to be a good change, but I feel like men are so often seen as better leaders even when the evidence says otherwise." This happens even though women have been shown to score higher than men on seventeen out of nineteen "capabilities that differ-entiate excellent leaders from average or poor ones." This includes the spheres we *expect* men to excel in, such as bold leadership.[7] And when communicating, we women have to be careful about our delivery and tone to make sure we aren't seen as too difficult or emotional. It puts us between a proverbial rock and hard place.

Women also tend to be more emotionally intelligent, which usually means the development of humility. Because of this, women in the US include fewer skills in their LinkedIn profiles than men who are in the same occupations and have the same amount of experience.[8] This has been dubbed the "humility gap."

Our podcast guest Jen Pestikas runs an organization called Brave Women at Work, where she helps women navigate their careers, get what they deserve, and do it all without burning out. She has firsthand experience of the high number of women who suffer from "imposter syndrome"—a condition that causes us to doubt our abilities and feel like a fraud. She says that even women who have reached management levels in business struggle with self-confidence and the courage to ask for what they want. "They're all so educated and experienced and have so much to offer," Jen says, "but then they come to me, and they're turned in on themselves. They're kind of broken."

Recently, Jen worked with a woman who was up for a nice promotion and who said she planned to ask for a 2 percent raise. When Jen was finished with her, the woman had the courage and negotiation skills to ask for 10 percent . . . and she got it! Jen believes women aren't expected to be brave or even develop courage because bravery is a traditionally masculine trait rather than a feminine one.

"Imposter syndrome becomes a self-fulfilling prophecy so that you start playing smaller," Jen says. "All of a sudden, you are acting out the part of the fearful, not competent working woman."

Do we *expect* women to be humbler than men, or is it just a by-product of overall societal gender expectations? We aren't sure, but if you're a woman, are you more humble than you need to be about your abilities? Maybe it's time to update that LinkedIn profile and give yourself the credit you deserve for all you've done and can do! If you're a stay-at-home mom, don't sell yourself short there, either. That requires mad skills!

## EXPECTATION: I HAVE TO BE SUPERWOMAN

Another of our podcast guests, Lucie Quigley, brought up the point that expectations of modern women are, to a large degree, even worse than in the past. She says we aren't just told we *can* have it all but that we *must* have it all. "I don't think there is much grace given to women anymore who want to be wives and mothers and be really good at it," she told us. We're supposed to have full-time jobs, carry the weight of home care, childcare, and elder care, while staying slim and looking fabulous. (Perfectionism again, anyone?) No wonder so many women suffer from imposter syndrome. Our expectations are of Wonder Woman proportions.

Erica Rooney told us on our podcast about what trying to have it all did to her. She is a successful C-suite executive as well as an energetic powerhouse of a coach, keynote speaker, and podcaster.

"I come from this generation where my mother taught me to be independent," Erica says. "But I also come from the generation where being a mom is your number one important role . . . I was chasing this proverbial 'all.' Being the perfect wife, the perfect mom, the perfect executive. Making sure that my kids had this picture-perfect Instagram life. And in reality, I was just breaking inside."

She had to take a step back and look at the unreasonable expectations she had placed on herself and give herself grace for being a human being. Like her, many of us need to take a breath and give ourselves a break. We could ask for help and stop trying to do everything ourselves. We could let the tasks that aren't so important just go. We could stop expecting so much of ourselves that we wind up exhausted. After all, we're people, not comic book characters.

## DO SAY "GAY" (IN FACT, SHOUT IT FROM THE ROOFTOPS!)

No chapter on gender would be worth its salt without a discussion of the impact gender expectations have on the LGBTQIA+ community. If you're part of this community, we don't have to tell you what that damage is like. But if you're straight and cisgender, it makes sense to check your expectations of people who have different gender identities from yours.

We find it sad when people are intolerant of anyone who diverges from our traditional images of male and female. Years ago, Keri was in a movie theater watching a romantic comedy in which two men kissed. Almost everyone in the audience said, "Ewww!" So when the female lead later kissed the male lead, she loudly screamed "Ewww" to make a point. We might chuckle at that story, but our gender expectations are especially serious for LGBTQIA+ people.

It seems obvious to the two of us that society is heading in the direction of accepting multiple gender identities, and fighting it is unkind and dangerous. We know people who grew up with gay parents and are straight themselves, and there truly is no such thing as a gay or transgender "agenda" that involves recruiting anybody. If we were that influenced by the sexuality or identity expectations of society, we would all be straight. If you fear that the mere existence of people with nontraditional gender identities or sexual orientations will do harm to you, we urge you to reconsider.

Our podcast guest Valerie Paris has firsthand knowledge of how awful it is to go through puberty as the gender that feels opposite to who you are. She was sixteen years old before she ever heard of transgender people. All she knew was that she was miserable. At that age, she assumed, "I'm just always going to be miserable, and I'm never going to know why."

Today, she is a highly successful transgender game designer with a background in marketing, community engagement, and immersive storytelling. Her latest games have focused on exploring themes of gender and LGBTQIA+ issues.

Valerie decided to transition when she asked herself: *If you could live your life how you'd want and do anything with no inhibitions, what would that look like? What would you really be?* These are great questions for all of us, especially to help us let go of restrictive roles and break out of our stuffy boxes. But no doubt these can be scary questions. Valerie avoided them most of her life because deep down, she knew the answer would be, "I'm a woman."

At the time she started her transition, Valerie was living as a man and working as head of marketing at a very corporate client-focused company. When word got out about the big decision, the boss called her in. She was sure she would be fired. "They can't have somebody like me as the face of their company talking to these clients," she thought.

But the opposite happened. The company president actually said, "I'm so happy for you." Valerie is aware that this is an extremely lucky and privileged position. She's the only transgender person most of her clients have ever met or worked with, so her goal is to help them see her as mostly just like everyone else, hopefully carving out a positive space for the next transgender person who crosses their paths. She hopes people will think, "Maybe they [transgender people] are just normal people who also work these kinds of jobs."

Still, whenever she meets with a client, there's no way to know how they will react. She wonders, "Is there a lurking racist transphobe in the ranks who's going to ruin my day? You never know."

The question that Valerie asked herself is immensely powerful. We'll ask it of you again before you finish reading this book, but right now, just begin to think about it: *If you could live your life how you'd want and do anything with no inhibitions, what would that look like?*

Meanwhile, please give your expectations of other gender identities some thought as well. We urge you to stay open and educate yourself as the conversation around these identities continues to evolve. While you may find yourself feeling uncomfortable if someone wants to be called "they" or if their name changes, we feel it's important to ask yourself: *Does this person's choice for their life truly affect me in mine?*

## NOTICE THE SUBTLE SEXISM (EVEN INSIDE YOUR OWN HEAD)

One of the things we've been doing is working on becoming more aware of our own unconscious gender biases that don't serve us or others. You might be so accustomed to some of your own that you don't notice them. So, we can all look for subtle sexism around us, including in our own words and actions.

For instance, how many movies and TV shows from just a few years ago are already cringe-worthy because of blatant sexism that we didn't notice at the time? Actress Molly Ringwald wrote an essay for *The New Yorker* in 2018 about the 1980s movies of the late screenwriter/director John Hughes in which she often starred. She admitted to mixed feelings about the way females were portrayed in the films, especially now that we're on the other side of the #MeToo movement. In the film *Sixteen Candles*, there's a scene in which a drunk girl is handed off to a guy she doesn't know, and she wakes up with that guy, assuming they had sex but with no memory of it. He asks her if she "enjoyed it," and she says, "I have this weird feeling I did." Even though she was treated like just a body who could be traded to any guy and used at will, the character was portrayed as someone who didn't realize she was being horribly objectified. And there was nothing in the script to indicate that it was wrong for the young men in the film to treat her that way.

Decades later, Molly asked the actress in that scene, Haviland Morris, how she felt about it. At first, Haviland felt the character was at least somewhat responsible since she got so drunk that she couldn't control what happened to her body. Yet, when Molly asked if she would feel that way if the character were her daughter, she conceded that no one is allowed to violate someone else's body without consent, period.[9] But it just goes to show how much even women have internalized sexism.

Here's a seemingly innocuous gender expectation that we might not notice without thinking about it. When Keri got pregnant with her son, she was working on her PhD. Meanwhile, her husband, Steve, as aforementioned, is an artist. Both men and women repeatedly asked her, "Do you think the baby will be an artist like your husband?" The assumption was that the child would take on the father's traits, not the mother's, because even today, a pregnant woman can still be seen (albeit unconsciously) as merely a baby-carrying vessel for whom a career is incidental.

Keri would answer, "Well, don't you think maybe the baby will be a PhD like their mom?"

Both men and women also asked her if she was planning to stay home after the baby was born, but no one asked Steve that question even though they knew Keri had the steady corporate job.

Keri is also often introduced by her first name, while a man with a PhD is more likely to be introduced as "Dr. So-and-so." This is true of politicians as well. Males are generally referred to by their last name, while females are frequently referred to by their first name. In a subtle but very real way, these practices infantilize and diminish women.

Don't even get us started about the practice of calling all men "Mr.," while women are often still referred to as "Miss" or "Mrs." We should all be called "Ms." because just like men, our marital status should be nobody's business. But these terms of address are a carryover from the days when women were considered property.

If you start to pay attention, you'll notice more and more of these subtle ways we keep outdated norms and gender expectations alive. Our friend Gwen began to notice how messages she'd absorbed when she was young she'd continued to impose on herself and others in her adulthood. "I started to see how I faded into the background in groups because I always thought that was what women were supposed to do," she says. "Then, I became aware of how often I judged other women for not living up to my narrow idea of how they 'should' act. I judged them for working after they had children or for deciding to stay single and not have children at all. It was hard to see these biases in myself, but I now realize they aren't fair. I was just reacting based on what I'd been taught, not what made sense. I have since broadened my idea of what a woman can be, and my life is easier because of it." Gwen now has a couple of dear friends who are single and child-free, and she speaks up more often in groups, unafraid to let her opinion be known. Her self-confidence has increased, and she is much more accepting of choices that differ from her own.

We try to pay attention when something doesn't feel right in terms of gender expectations, whether it's happening to us or someone around us. When we aren't sure, we talk to others we trust to get their perspective. You may begin to notice, for example, how men are often encouraged to only express anger and no other emotions. Men, if you see a woman being treated unfairly, speak up if you can. Men *and* women, consider speaking up if you see someone gay, transgender, or gender nonconforming being mistreated or discriminated against. Besides casting off the gender expectations placed on ourselves, we can raise awareness by calling out biases when we see them. While it may feel daunting to say something, it can make a big difference to people in the LGBTQIA+ community. You might just say, "You may not realize it, but that could be hurtful" or "Doesn't it make sense to be kind to others? We don't all have to be the same."

Meanwhile, we can offer more grace and generosity to *anyone* who tries to break tired gender expectations (including ourselves). If you're working to break out of a gender box, or you accidentally fall into one related to gender norms, give yourself a break while you work on your *break OUT*. Whether you're in a box or not, it helps us all to stay informed on the current conversations. Wherever you sit on the spectrum, we are all affected by gender expectations.

## Ask Yourself: Gender Expectations

Now it's time to look at the gender expectations that may have caused a problem in your own life. You've been given lots of examples throughout the chapter that you may never have considered before. As a result, you might need to revise the gender box that you created at the end of chapter 1. After having read this chapter, do you think this box should remain the same, or should it be smaller or larger than you originally thought?

If you're flying free on the outside, that's fantastic! Unfortunately, if you're female, chances are you aren't.

As you did at the end of the previous two chapters, think about how you've been expected to act, but this time, based on your perceived gender. What gender expectations do you remember from your childhood, and how have they shaped you? If you had both a mother and father figure, how did they act? Did they fall into traditional gender roles? Do you still adhere to these expectations, and do you feel any of them have been or remain harmful to you? If so, in what ways? For example, you might realize, like Gwen did, that being a woman made you feel you ought to remain quiet, and so you didn't speak up for yourself. As a result, maybe you've allowed other people to assert what they want while staying silent about your own preferences and desires. If you're a man, you may recall that your father was very stoic, rarely showing any emotion at all, and you emulated him in spite of yourself, thinking that's how a man is supposed to act.

How have gender expectations played a part in your career? If you're a woman, have you experienced workplace discrimination, either in terms of pay or advancement, or as a mother? If you're male, have you been expected to work long hours even though you're a father?

What gender expectations have you experienced in romantic relationships or friendships? For example, if you're a woman, have you been expected to always dress or act feminine? Have you observed that some men seem uncomfortable if you're ambitious or accomplished? If you're a man, have women expected you to be ambitious and accomplished, or have they expected you to always initiate sex or immediately pay the check at dinner?

What gender expectations have you noticed in other areas of your life such as in your religious life and in your community?

If you stopped abiding by these gender expectations, how would your life look?

When you feel you have unearthed some of the gender expectations that have held you back, write down the one that you feel is boxing you in the most, whether it is inflicted on you by other people or by yourself. How much wider and more open would your box be if you let go of this expectation? If you weren't afraid of the consequences, would you immediately let go of this most consequential gender expectation? Don't forget to hold on to what you write!

# CHAPTER 5
# Where You Came From Matters

Kelly was stunned by the grocery cashier's chattiness the first time she bought food after moving to Los Angeles. *Wow, cashiers were never this talkative at the Piggy Wiggly in Milwaukee!* she thought. She soon discovered this is the norm in Southern California, while in Wisconsin, people would huff and puff if a cashier dared delay them with idle chitchat.

The two of us often laugh about the differences between the Midwest and LA. Now, after living in California for a few years, when we come across an unusually quiet person behind the cash register, the first impulse is to ask, "Are you okay?"

Sure, these are generalizations, but there's no denying that there are cultural differences, whether between countries, regions, cities/towns, neighborhoods, or other geographical groups. For example, anyone who has taken a train in Germany and then in Italy can attest to the cultural differences experienced there. The trains in Germany have run on the same tracks for decades and are pretty much always on time. In Italy, it seems it's anyone's guess when a train will leave or what track it will depart from, and you'll probably find out four minutes before you have to sprint to catch it. And cultural differences can show up just as easily between two adjacent small towns as between two countries.

As long as we don't impose our expectations on each other, our cultural differences can be wonderful, can't they? Who wants everyone to be the same? Travel and food would be boring as hell. Cultural diversity makes life interesting. We wouldn't have fondue, burritos, and sushi. Or Chopin, hip-hop, and mambo. Or Tudor palaces, Roman coliseums, and pagodas. Part of the excitement of going to another region or country is to see how their customs differ from our own. Even in our home countries, most cities and towns have restaurants offering a variety of cuisines. We wouldn't experience that if everyone insisted on sticking to their own cultural preferences and idiosyncrasies.

Some cultural differences are fun and funny like the chatty versus quiet grocery store cashiers, while others keep our lives smaller than we'd like. As always, the question is: do these expectations suit the real you, or do they keep you in a box and prevent you from doing what you want in your life?

In our quest to peel the onion of expectations from family systems to religions to gender norms, we couldn't possibly leave out how cultural and regional expectations can also put us in little boxes. In other words, where you came from matters in terms of what's expected of you and what you might expect of yourself without realizing it.

Since we're American, we'll explore some of the common expectations from within our own borders. Not that we're putting down the US. We're proud to live in this country. Heck, the fact that we can write this book is due to our freedom of speech, and we know not everyone in the world has that privilege. But freedoms and privileges can include some expectations that put a fair amount of pressure on us.

Let's talk about a couple of those, as well as a key regional expectation and a common cultural expectation that might come from both our family and community. If you are from another country outside the United States, we invite you to consider some of the cultural expectations you encounter there and how they have influenced your own life.

## EXPECTATION: THE AMERICAN DREAM MEANS LOTS OF MONEY, STATUS, AND A BIG HOUSE

Isn't this the land of equal opportunity, and can't we all make it if we just pull ourselves up by our bootstraps? You might ask yourself, "If 'anyone' is supposed to be able to make it here, why am I struggling so much?" We still have a belief in this country that the American Dream means earning a degree from a prestigious college, earning a lot of money, and owning a big house. Otherwise, we don't see ourselves as successful. (And if someone *is* very successful, they have permission to be an asshole. Just look at how much we excuse bad billionaire behavior!)

Plus, let's face it: we don't all start on equal footing by a long shot, so it isn't so easy to "pull yourself up by your bootstraps." (What are bootstraps anyway?) This isn't to say that you can't make your wildest dreams come true. We're here to tell you that you can, and we know lots of people who have! But not everyone starts from the same place, and the question we're asking is: are those dreams yours, or are they based on the American Dream mythology? Some of us end up chasing a goal that may have nothing to do with what would actually make us happy, and each of us has to define success and happiness on a personal level beyond cultural experiences.

Our country can be like the pageant mom, forcing us to always work, always make money, and always try to be the winner. This can be an exhausting race with no finish line.

We met a man named Andrzej who told us about his grandparents, who immigrated to New York just before World War II broke out. They brought their knowledge of the dry-cleaning business from Europe and opened their first storefront on the Lower East Side of Manhattan in the late 1930s. A decade later, it had become a thriving family business and they owned a chain of dry cleaners throughout the city.

"My family certainly had a work ethic in Poland," Andrzej says, "but their love of America and what it provided them meant hard work times ten. In order to be worthy of the American Dream, all of us kids were expected to go to the best schools and push ourselves to the nth degree. We had to constantly feed the beast, which was this belief that we had to prove we were number one, just like our family's adopted country. We had been given lots of privileges, and we had to take advantage of every single one. Otherwise, we were squandering this opportunity."

Andrzej's parents bought into this expectation hook, line, and sinker, but for the grandchildren who were born in America, it started to feel like its own brand of oppression. They had watched their parents work long hours and make sacrifices to put their kids through Ivy League colleges, encouraging them to become white-collar professionals who hired others to run the family dry-cleaning business.

"Don't get me wrong," Andrzej says, "we were so fortunate, and we absolutely do honor this great country that gave our family the chances it has had. At the same time, it was a lot to live up to. I, for one, reacted by dropping out of college after two years. This was a scandal in our family, but it wasn't until I could relax this expectation and think about what I truly wanted for myself that I was able to go back to school and finish my degree."

Our country may be great, but that doesn't mean each of us can be great every day of our lives. It also doesn't mean we have to always be "the best." We can relax our expectations of ourselves and settle for "good enough," at least some of the time. And maybe we do what we think will make us happy as Andrzej did rather than subscribe to the myth of the American Dream or do what others expect of us. Maybe that means starting over, like a woman we met named Paulette.

"I bought into the whole American Dream thing and became an accountant at a big CPA firm because I was convinced I needed the big house," she says. "While I was saving up for the down payment, it was my wife, Tamra, who finally opened my eyes. She told me one day that no house was worth working myself to death."

So Paulette got a job that didn't require such long, stressful hours. This would mean that she and Tamra would only be able to afford a modest house at best. But they were both much happier for it.

"I discovered that my personal version of the American Dream wasn't big at all," she says. "Success for me meant less pressure, time to spend with my family, and actually enjoying my work, even if it also meant a less extravagant lifestyle. I didn't have to be number one or live in a big house to be happy."

If you find that you're holding on to some expectation that you must be the "best" or have what you consider to be the "best" in order to be happy, it's worth examining what would truly give you a fulfilled life. Striving to always be on top can be stressful and difficult to maintain, so it's worth asking yourself why it's important to you. We're asking you to examine whether your vision of success is knotted up in this expectation of what a successful life is *supposed* to look like instead of what it organically looks like for you.

## "I HAVE TO DO IT MYSELF"

The US is quite individualistic, which means we sometimes expect to do everything on our own without help. But without the assistance we need, this expectation can keep us from achieving what we want, and it can keep us separated from others if we let it.

We could perhaps learn a thing or two from people who live in Blue Zones, regions that were identified and researched by Dan Buettner, author of *The Blue Zones: 9 Lessons for Living Longer from the People Who've Lived the Longest*. Scientists found that one of the reasons for the longevity of people who live in Blue Zones is their connection with their communities, including how much they help each other.

Of course, we aren't saying that Americans never help one another. Nothing could be further from the truth. But in 2023, the U.S. Surgeon General released a report called "Our Epidemic of Loneliness and Isolation,"[1] pointing out that a lack of social connection can indeed contribute to some of our most common diseases and shorten our lives.

So we could stand to relax our American individualism that tells us we have to do it all by ourselves. Counting on our community can be a strength rather than a weakness.

## EXPECTATION: WE DON'T DO THAT AROUND THESE PARTS

Even in the same country, from one state to the next, from one town to the next, from one community to the next, cultural expectations may differ. And like the grocery store experiences that we had when we first moved to California, they can trip us up when we travel or move someplace new. They can also place us into smothering boxes if we aren't careful.

Our experience in the Midwest, for instance, is that people don't like it if you're too assertive. They're more likely to be passive, if not passive-aggressive. If you're direct, they might say something like, "Oh, you must be from New York," which is *not* a compliment, by the way. The implication is "We don't do that around these parts."

Our friend moved to New York City from Kentucky and had to learn how to be assertive. Because of her upbringing, she had no idea how to stand up for herself. Now people in the Midwest and the South think she's a bit abrupt because she has adopted a more straightforward, "New York City" way of communicating. Of course, she was under no obligation to adopt the more assertive New York attitude when she moved there, but she felt it actually suited her better than being more passive. "Some people prefer to be quiet, and that's great for them if it works," she says. "But me? What's natural for my personality is to be outspoken and honest when it makes sense, and NYC gave me permission to express the real me."

Keri had a similar experience. Within the city of Chicago, she felt she could be her full assertive self without anyone blinking an eye. After taking that Chicago attitude (bolder and sassier with plenty of swear words) to Milwaukee, people frequently asked her, "Are you a Chicago lawyer?" Again, *not* a compliment.

Culture also determines how we relate to time—like the example of trains in Germany versus Italy. In some parts of the country and the world, time is more fluid, while in other places, people are expected to be prompt. "In the Midwest, it wasn't uncommon to start meetings at 8:00 a.m.," Kelly says. "The West Coast seems to be more laid back about time, so in California, we start at 8:30 a.m. or more likely 9:00 a.m."

In a place where more people tend to be religious, the first question might be "What church do you go to?" In more secular places, that question is unlikely to come up even during a long conversation.

While it's natural for a community to establish unspoken cultural rules, if those rules make the walls of our cultural expectation box close in on who we are, we need to look for ways to honor our individuality while also integrating into our community. It isn't always easy, so you may have to think hard about it. Which cultural expectations fit you, and which ones don't? Of the ones that don't fit you, are they important enough to you to defy them or at least push the envelope? Sometimes, by pushing matters a little bit, you can get the people around you to open their mind to other perspectives. Other times, you might move to a new place only to find that the cultural differences are too much for you.

That happened to Veronica, a friend's sister, who moved from Montana to Chicago for a job that initially sounded like a dream.

She was used to the cold weather, and she enjoyed being able to go to the grocery store on the way home from work rather than driving a half hour to the nearest store. But the fast rhythm of Chicago was hard for her to get used to. She even found it hard to adjust to the speed with which people spoke. She felt that she got lost in the crowd, and she missed the wide-open spaces of her home state. "I hoped I would get used to it," Veronica says, "but after giving it almost two years, I had a conversation with my mother, who pointed out how miserable I sounded. So I moved back to Montana, where the rhythm of the place is my rhythm. It just suits me better."

It's up to you to decide if you can handle a particular culture or not, and self-awareness (yes, again) is key. The better you know yourself, the more you'll know what's right for you and what isn't.

Of course, there are extreme cases in which a community isn't welcoming to certain people, such as LGBTQIA+ individuals or people of color.

Just as religious differences can cause us to fear or even hate people who aren't like us, cultural expectations can sometimes keep us from accepting each other, especially when we've never been face-to-face with those we perceive to be different. When we actually meet them, we're more likely to see our commonalities rather than our cultural distinctions.

Such was the case when Black blues musician Daryl Davis started spending time with Ku Klux Klan members. He met with more than a hundred of them, and when he was done, more than two-thirds left the KKK, even though he never tried to convince them to leave. This is what psychologists call "contact theory," which basically says that when we meet each other, we sometimes find out we aren't so different after all, even if we're from a different race, culture, or religion. When we're face-to-face, it's easier to see that even though we might have some different ideas and behaviors, we aren't just a collection of negative stereotypes. We're all human beings who want to love and be loved, and we want to find happiness for ourselves and our loved ones.

## EXPECTATION: WE'VE ALWAYS DONE IT THIS WAY

The opening song of the Broadway musical *Fiddler on the Roof* is called "Tradition." It sets up the conflict that will arise as the younger characters want to challenge some of the traditions that the older characters have long held dear.

Many cultural traditions can be handed down for generations, and even though the US is nearly 250 years old, plenty of those traditions from our ancestors' countries are still strong within our families. We might be expected to follow them even if they don't sit well with who we are. The "we've always done it this way" expectation can squeeze the walls of our cultural expectation box until we gasp for air.

For example, the authors of one of our favorite books, *Riding the Waves of Culture: Understanding Diversity in Global Business*, pinpointed that some cultures tend to be more emotionally neutral, while others tend to be more expressive.[2] A hotel manager in Austria told a friend of ours that it isn't customary in their culture to greet and welcome hotel guests in an effusively friendly way. So, they had to train their personnel to smile broadly and actively welcome guests because it's what American tourists and business travelers expect. Their more neutral reserve, normal to them, might seem to Americans to be cold or rude. It's similar to what we experienced with our grocery checkers in Wisconsin versus Los Angeles. Obviously, Americans are generally thought to be more emotional than neutral, but emotionality varies a lot depending on where you are in the country.

Learning that tidbit about Austrian tradition was no surprise to us because both of us grew up in German-American families whose members weren't emotionally demonstrative. Keri's family didn't hug, for example. When she made friends with a woman from a Polish-American family, she was exposed to regular hugging for the first time. It has had a very positive impact on her, making her more open and affectionate in her life. But despite having studied international communications, it took her some time to get used to it.

"Acceptable emotions in our family were anger, disappointment, and shame," Keri says. "Joy was meh . . . except when you were drinking, of course."

Kelly says her family was similar. "Work had to be done before you could think about playing," she says. "My family often celebrated a sense of accomplishment that came from waking up early and tackling projects. And early was considered 'on time.'"

We have found our German-American cultural traditions to be a bit too structured for how we want to be. By learning to loosen up, we've been able to fly out of our restrictive cultural expectation boxes and enjoy our lives more. But we don't feel the need to require anybody else to be like us. Some people like structure and routine, which is just fine as long as they don't get pissed off when the rest of us may not be as structured or routine-driven. (If we're five minutes late, please give us a break!)

The expectation becomes a problem when we adhere to that "we've always done it this way" attitude without any openness to change. And that rigidity might also make us intolerant of each other's differences just as the expectation that "we don't do that around these parts" did. So we recommend relaxing the expectation that all traditions must be maintained. Keep the ones that work, and create new ones when the old ones have passed their expiration date.

## UNCONSCIOUS BIAS

All of us have a tendency to expect people to behave the way we learned how to behave growing up, and it can be difficult for us to accept people with different cultural traditions and expectations. We all—and we mean *all*—have unconscious biases. (Of course, the two of us have gotten rid of all of our biases because we've done the work. Just kidding! Of course, we have biases. When we said "all of us," we really did mean *all*.)

Every single one of us could benefit from increasing our awareness of our unconscious biases so that we become more tolerant of each other's differences.

Psychologists have identified more than a hundred different kinds of unconscious biases—way too many for us to talk about here—and you don't have to educate yourself about all of them. Let's just talk about three of the most common ones that you've probably experienced yourself, whether you've fallen prey to it from the outside or within.

First, there's "confirmation bias." This describes our tendency to look for information that or people who confirm the beliefs we already have. For example, when we only read newspapers that align with our political views. This bias can cause us to interpret information through the filter of what we already believe and prevent us from recognizing faulty thinking.

The "halo effect" bias causes us to assume someone has many positive qualities based on just one quality that we perceive as positive. Did you know that most US presidents have been tall? This is because we tend to think tall people are good leaders. Weird, right? Because what's height got to do with it (got to do, got to do with it)?

Then, there's "similar-to-me" bias, which we want to talk about a little more than the others. This one says we're likely to be positively biased toward people we perceive as similar to us. Natural, right? The problem occurs when it prevents us from meeting people who are different, as with the Ku Klux Klan members who had never actually met a Black person.

Here's a less extreme example: White people don't tend to watch movies where the main character or most of the characters are of another race. This is because they don't perceive that characters of other races are like them, and it's been studied enough to have a name—the "ingroup bias." That's one of the reasons why the 2023 Academy Award Best Picture winner, *Everything Everywhere All at Once*, is so unusual (and hopefully a sign of more to come). It's one of the few films that has been successful with all audiences even though it features a mostly Asian-American cast. Underrepresented groups, on the other hand, haven't had much choice but to watch movies about white people. Historically, there haven't been many other options.

Our friend Portia noticed the racial empathy gap in herself and decided to do something about it. "It dawned on me that I never saw movies with main characters of other races or nationalities, so I purposely started watching them," she says. "I watched African American films and foreign films from non-European countries. I discovered that I identified with all of them, and I loved it. Now,

I'm a huge foreign film buff, and I also make sure I watch American films that are about groups other than my own. This alone has really broadened my perspective and made me want to seek out a more diverse group of friends, too."

It's safe and easy to stick with the familiar. Again, we aren't judging it as wrong, but it's something to think about and decide if you want to explore people and places that are different. Jacquelyn Adams, a training and development manager and freelance writer, told us on our podcast about her experience in the Peace Corps. She worked in a rural village in a developing country where they had no running water or electricity. "This opened my eyes to so many different ways of life, and I think it kind of embedded in me this curiosity and this ability to question what I had previously considered was the norm. And made me open to taking more risk and allowing myself to be a little bit scared sometimes or being a little bit put off-balance."

We found this so inspiring. Nobody likes feeling scared or off-balance, but it's hard to learn or grow when we stay in our comfort zone all the time. As another podcast guest, Janet Livingstone, executive coach and founder of Culture Is Key, put it, meeting people from other cultures shakes up our expectations and how we view our traditions. We don't realize how many cultural traditions we follow until we experience another culture with very different ones. "Then, we can see our own society with so much more clarity and perspective," she says. "Unless we see something different and live with something different, we can't know ourselves fully."

We have also felt off-balance when we've been in situations where we were part of the underrepresented group. As white people in the US, we don't feel underrepresented often, but when we do, it gives us a sense of what it's like for so many people who aren't in the majority on a regular basis. It jars us out of our normal state of privilege, which we have found to be a valuable way of rattling loose some of those tenacious biases.

In whatever way you do it, we recommend challenging yourself to examine your biases, expectations, and traditions. You can not only stop yourself from putting other people in boxes but stop putting yourself in them as well. You might also start to recognize the biases, prejudices, and expectations that are imposed on others so that you can call them out and stand up for fairness and justice.

## LIFE GOALS: INDIVIDUALITY AND TOLERANCE

While we don't want an awareness of cultural differences to cause us to stereotype people and therefore put them in the very boxes we're trying to break out of, awareness of our differences can help us in two ways: first, we can better recognize the cultural expectations that we want to put aside, and second, we can realize that our differences are usually to be celebrated rather than feared. We can use that awareness to become more accepting and tolerant of each other, as well as more curious than judgmental.

And when we visit someone else's culture, we abide by and respect their rules (as long as those expectations aren't hurtful to anyone).

When we're flexible back home, we hold on to the expectations that work for us and let other people do the same, as long as no one is harmed or forced to abide by what doesn't work for them. It's a balancing act, but it's more harmonious when we can adopt a "live and let live" attitude rather than insisting it's "our way or the highway" for everybody.

One of the reasons we wanted to write this book is that we imagine a world where compassion for one another is the prevalent choice we make when we confront our differences. Doesn't that sound like a nice place to be?

Inevitably, you will love some of the traditions of your culture, while you will find that observing others keeps you in a box that's way too stuffy. Let's explore some of the unwanted expectations in your life that have their roots in culture.

## Ask Yourself: Cultural Expectations

Now that you've read this chapter, take a look at the box you created at the end of chapter 1 for your community and culture. Was it small, medium, large, or nonexistent? After reading this chapter, do you need to change it?

If you grew up in a community or culture that differs from where you live now, what expectations do you recall from that time? Did you feel like you belonged in the community or communities where you grew up, or did you feel like an outsider? If you have moved around a lot, make note of the different expectations (maybe even contradictory ones) that you have felt in the various places.

Are there any expectations from the communities/cultures where you grew up that you are still adhering to? Do these expectations fit who you are now, and do they make sense for you? Or are you still following them out of habit? For example, if your culture was extremely polite, has this held you back from being as outgoing and fun-loving as you would like to be?

Have you diverged from the expectations in your community

at any point in your life? If so, how have the people around you reacted, and how did that feel? How comfortable do you feel about acting differently from how people around you expect? Is it easy or difficult for you? Write about some experiences you've had in which you went against the cultural/community grain.

When you have unearthed some of the cultural expectations that may have held you back, write down the one that you feel has been the most influential and consequential in your life. Which one is boxing you in the most, whether it is inflicted on you by other people or your own expectations of yourself based on culture/community?

If you stop abiding by the most consequential expectation on your list, how will your life look? What will be different? How much wider and more open would your box be?

If you weren't afraid of the consequences, would you immediately let go of this particular expectation?

# CHAPTER 6
# Don't Worry—You Will Find a Nice Person to Marry

*When are you going to settle down and get married?*

*When are you going to have kids?*

*Now that you've had one child, don't you want another . . . and another?*

Sometimes, it seems like the marriage and family expectations never end, right? If we're single, people expect us to get married, and if we're married, they expect us to have kids. If we have one kid, they expect us to have *more* kids. Gahhhhhhh! Can't we just live our lives as we want?

Of course we can. Unfortunately, a lot of us allow ourselves to be stuck in one of those little boxes again—this time with regard to marital and parental status. When it comes to marriage, our society (and many societies around the world) is prone to expectations about what we "should" do. If we diverge from those expectations, we usually get a lot of questions and some significant side-eye. From some family members and friends, we get outright pressure. In this chapter, we'll talk about the expectations not just to get married and have kids, but the ones about who we marry, how our wedding should look, and more.

## EXPECTATION: DON'T YOU WANT TO SPEND YOUR LIFE WITH SOMEONE?

If you're single, be glad you aren't in Denmark. Unmarried twenty-five-year-olds are apparently tied to a chair while their friends throw cinnamon at them. (We don't get it either, but it's supposedly from some old tradition involving spice traders who *forgot* to get married.) The Danish get off easy, though, compared to the German tradition, where they even have their own dang festival for unmarried women when they near twenty-five. (What is it about the age of twenty-five?) That festival is called Schachtelfest, which translates, believe it or not, to "old box." We don't know about you, but we're insulted for every German woman who has ever existed.[1]

We may not have such rituals in the US, but how many times have single people been told—with heavy doses of condescension and pity—that they shouldn't give up? If they just keep trying and give it time, they'll find the perfect partner and be able to settle down. The assumption is, of course, that single people (at least single women) *want* to get married. We don't *expect* them to choose to stay single. Why would a female person not want to be coupled? Surely, she's lying if she says she doesn't want marriage. Right?

Well, it turns out that more than half of American women (52 percent) are single, and there are 20 percent more women who have never been married than there were a decade ago. According to a 2018 Tinder survey, and contrary to what you might think, more women than men said they appreciated the benefits of being single.[2]

Like many others who choose to remain unmarried, Kelly is content with her career, friendships, and freedom. "My son sees Kelly and says she's killing it with her business, her home, her dog, and her full life," Keri says of her bestie. "She isn't a lonely person. She doesn't listen to society's message that her single life can't be 100 percent great."

But Kelly definitely had to contend with the expectations of others. "When I was younger, in my twenties and thirties, I found that I was asked questions more frequently than today," she says. People asked: *Are you seeing anyone? Don't you want to date? You're okay being alone?* Or they made assumptions and said things like: *There's someone out there for you! You should try online dating.*

"After a while," Kelly says, "I got used to navigating the myriad questions. I used the same answer, 'I'm really happy with my life the way it is.' I didn't feel the need to over-explain, go into detail, or justify my reasons. It's truly no one's business, just as it isn't my business to ask why someone chose to get married or have children."

Kelly's rebellious grandmother was a role model for her in this respect. "She lost her husband when she was young," Kelly says. "But my grandma was in a relationship with a man for years, and they lived in separate homes. When people asked her if they were going to get married, she said, 'Absolutely not!' She was sometimes asked if she was worried about what people would say. Her answer was, 'I don't care what they say. I live my life.'"

Kelly finds singlehood liberating, as she can live on her own terms. "Not once have I questioned my decision," she says. "I lead a fulfilling life, and I'm thankful for it. When I come home each day, for example, the house is exactly how I left it. No surprises!" She has strong relationships that provide her with plenty of love and connection, and she loves that she's free to be on her own or have company whenever she chooses.

"When people find out I'm single," Kelly says, "some have told me in a hushed tone that they wish they hadn't gotten married, like it's their dirty little secret." Our friend Bonnie, now seventy-seven years old, is a case in point. She gave in to the pressure and got married at age twenty-two. "I was so immature at that age that I had no idea what I was doing," she says. "All the girls around me started getting married by eighteen. So my parents pressured me, my peers pressured me, and even the community pressured me. Meanwhile, a part of me dreamed of traveling the world and photographing people, exotic places, and wild animals, but that dream seemed impossible." She married a young man who appeared to be "nice enough" and had three children with him before she was thirty. "I think my husband, Pete, was just giving in to societal pressure too," Bonnie says. "We were two kids playing house, and our children have the emotional scars to show for that."

When she turned forty-six, Bonnie had an emotional breakdown. The pressure of living up to everyone else's expectations had taken a terrible toll on her. "I just couldn't keep up the façade," she admits. "Pete and I had a nasty divorce, but later, we were able to become friends again. Once I was feeling better, I finally began to study photography. My work started to get some attention, and by age fifty-two, I was on assignment in parts of Africa to take photos of the people, exotic places, and wild animals I had longed to see when I was young. Two of my children have been supportive, but one of my daughters thinks I've lost my mind. Being single took some getting used to, but I have come to prefer it. The bottom line is I'm finally happy with myself and my life." We think Bonnie rocks!

Marriage can be wonderful *if* it's what you truly want. But if you're single, we recommend being honest with yourself. What do you think will *truly* make *you* happy, not your parents, grandparents, siblings, or friends—only you? The consequences of living someone else's life are significant and can even impact future generations, as Bonnie noted.

Choosing to go against the grain takes courage, so if you do it, be proud of yourself. When you get unsolicited feedback or questions (and you will), stand in your truth, and answer honestly if you wish . . . but only if you wish. You don't owe anyone an explanation for *your* life choices. Or you could even throw the question right back at them: *Why didn't* you *choose to stay single?*

You can also be an ally for others who have chosen a nontraditional lifestyle. "In my life, I have been surrounded by parents who have been married for more than forty years, family and friends who have great marriages, and friends who have always been single or stayed single after divorce," Kelly says. "Regardless of their relationship status, their choices are uniquely theirs and only theirs to make. It's important that we all be allies for one another and support each other in living our best lives."

Besides the expectation that we get married in the first place, there are so many expectations around the wedding ritual that families sometimes suffer permanent rifts because of them.

## WHAT'S WITH ALL THE WEDDING EXPECTATIONS?

If you follow any advice column, you'll see countless stories of people who are fighting with family members over wedding expectations. Many engaged couples don't realize they have the right to decide *everything* with regard to their own wedding. Instead, they listen to what their parents or friends want. All too often, they end up with a wedding they hate. If it isn't their day, whose is it supposed to be? In our opinion, nobody's but theirs.

That's the way Keri and her husband, Steve, decided to do it. "I wasn't a little girl who grew up dreaming of weddings," Keri says. "I was never the girl with bridal magazines and a vision board. So when we talked about our wedding, I told Steve I thought most traditional wedding stuff was bullshit."

She had been to a friend's huge wedding and thought it felt impersonal and over the top—like a machine. She had also talked to other friends who regretted letting outside influences affect their wedding. So she suggested they get married in Las Vegas. Steve asked, "Are you serious?" But he loved the idea.

Some of their friends had proclaimed they were having a "week of love" before they got married, which made both Keri and Steve want to barf. It sounded like a trite romantic comedy, so they laughed as they decided to call their wedding week "a week of debauchery." (Truthfully, they just spent some time at the Grand Canyon, but that label fit them better than a "week of love" ever would. They got married in Las Vegas in front of an Elvis impersonator and about forty friends. After the ceremony, they all went to the Luxor Hotel & Casino buffet and a nightclub with go-go dancers in cages, where they danced until 2:00 a.m. (That was as debauched as it got.) Their seventy-five-year-old friend was still dancing and drinking lemon-drop shots when they left. (She was the most debauched of them all.)

Keri and Steve expected their married friends to be appalled by the story of their eccentric wedding, but instead, most of them sighed and said, "That sounds great. I wish we had done that."

Their weddings were for someone else, and many of them felt the big money they spent wasn't worth it.

To make Keri's wedding even less conventional, she wore a black dress with purple lace that she found in a shop in New Orleans. Where did the white dress tradition come from anyway?

It turns out that many of the wedding traditions we see as so important are in place for downright silly reasons. The white wedding dress didn't become a tradition until 1840, when Queen Victoria decided to wear a champagne-colored gown. With no photography at the time, the illustrations of her dress looked white, and since everybody wanted to look like a royal, the white wedding dress became a thing. Of course, white is also associated with purity, as if the majority of women getting married today are *pure* in the virginal sense. Give us a break! As Keri said when she chose her black and purple dress, "The white wedding dress expectation is patriarchal and dumb."

Before Queen Victoria's purported white dress, it was customary for brides to wear a variety of colors. In fact, red was one of the most popular, which is still true in parts of Asia.[3]

Most people know that veils date back to the times of arranged marriages when the groom wasn't allowed to see the bride's face until after he had already said his vows.

Don't even get us started about the tradition of the diamond engagement ring. While the wedding ring itself is a much older tradition that started in Egypt and signifies eternity, the tradition of the diamond engagement ring is even younger than the white wedding dress. Before the 1930s, engagement rings could have any stone in them. But then a copywriter came up with the slogan "A Diamond Is Forever," for the diamond company De Beers. It remains one of the most successful ad campaigns in history. De

Beers manipulated the market to make it seem like diamonds were rare, and thus, better than other gems, an utterly bogus claim. In fact, diamonds are hard to resell because they're so common, and there's a stockpile of them at diamond companies.

De Beers is also responsible for the "two-month rule" that says men have to spend the equivalent of two months' salary on the engagement ring. It's nothing more than a scam to manipulate people into parting with more of their hard-earned money. Meanwhile, the diamond mining industry is tremendously ugly. If you ever want to know the awful truth about it, read *The Heartless Stone: A Journey Through the World of Diamonds, Deceit, and Desire* by Tom Zoellner.[4]

Then there's the tradition of a woman taking the man's last name. This one comes from the time when women were considered their husband's possession, but the truth is that most of us have a man's last name no matter what. Even if we don't take our husband's when we get married, we probably still have our father's last name. For some women who had a less-than-happy relationship with their father, it's preferable to take the name of a man they choose.

For Keri, taking her husband's last name was strictly a practical matter. Her mother had three last names—her so-called maiden name (another outdated term if ever there was one), Keri's father's last name, and her second husband's last name. "It caused a lot of confusion and hassle," Keri says. "So I didn't take my husband's name because I felt obligated to do it. I did it because I wanted simplicity in my life. I made a conscious choice."

The origin of the phrase "I now pronounce you man and wife" is the same as why the woman takes the man's last name—woman as possession. The male member of the partnership gets to stay a *man*, while the woman loses her autonomy and becomes solely a *wife* (i.e., property). Thankfully, more wedding ceremonies are now using "I now pronounce you husband and wife," but it's appalling that anyone is still using the antiquated marriage pronouncement.

The bottom line is that most of these traditions were either made up or date back to when women had few, if any, rights.

Of course, as with all of the topics in this book, it isn't our intention to convince anyone to do anything our way. All we're encouraging you to do is ask yourself what you truly want and make your plans without worrying about the expectations of your family, friends, or society. It's useful to even question your own expectations and whether they serve you. If, for example, you always thought you'd spend a lot of money on a huge wedding, is that what you actually want, or do you feel like you *should* want it? Do you feel your fiancé doesn't love you enough unless they give you a huge diamond engagement ring? If so, where does that belief come from, and does it make sense? If you decide you absolutely want to be married and have a big blowout wedding in a white lace dress with a giant rock on your finger, we'll be the first to cheer you on. We just urge you to be true to you and your partner, first and foremost.

## WEDDING EXPECTATIONS ARE CHILD'S PLAY COMPARED TO MARRIAGE EXPECTATIONS

We tend to have tons of expectations about the marital relationship itself. These can be serious enough to get us into real trouble (even divorce, if we aren't careful). We can get so caught up in our love that realism flies out the window, but it will fly right back in soon enough when we're down to the nitty-gritty of living together day by day. So, it's helpful to think about your expectations ahead of time and have an open and honest conversation with your partner-to-be in an effort to avoid misunderstandings. Here are just a few expectations we thought you might want to consider and discuss:

1. *We expect to be compatible even if our values don't align.* Our podcast guest Amy Evans, the founder of AlignWomen, a leadership and networking organization for professional women, and the host of The AlignWomen podcast, emphasized the importance of making sure that our values align before we commit to another person. "Before we were married," she told us, "[my husband and I] discovered that when we clarified our values to each other, it helped us untangle some sticky communication issues." They realized, for example, that she places a higher value on privacy than her husband does, while he has a strong need for connection with others. That desire to connect sometimes led him to share personal details with people that made Amy uncomfortable. Since they had both taken the time to evaluate their personal core values and opted to talk about them with each other, they were able to clearly understand and respect their differences. It may take some work to come to an agreement when your values don't align perfectly, but the only way to reconcile them is to first be aware of them and then communicate them.

We tend to plan weddings but not marriages, and we might ask more questions of a potential roommate than a potential mate. When we don't ask important questions before we get hitched, we might be in for a rude awakening. What do we expect of each other once we're married and living together? What do we expect if we have children? Do we assume our hot sex life will continue forever, or can we survive the end of the honeymoon period (which typically only lasts about two years)? All too often, we're afraid to have these conversations because we think it could mean the end of the relationship. But better to know beforehand than possibly suffer years of misery.

Our friend knew a therapist who confessed to her that he and his fiancée had never discussed whether they wanted to have children. Their wedding was just two weeks away when they finally sat down to talk about the important stuff. Guess what? After everything was paid for, they had to call off the wedding because they realized they didn't want the same things.

2. *We expect ourselves and/or our partner to fill traditional gender roles.* A friend told us about a couple—Beth and Jason—who had been together for two years. After they got married and moved in together, Beth began to wonder if she'd made the wrong decision. It had never dawned on her that Jason's history of having a professional cleaner for his apartment and always sending his laundry out for washing might have implications for her. His parents had never required him to help with the cleaning, and since he could afford it, he just paid somebody else to do it. But guess who became the "professional" cleaner when they were in the same space and could no longer afford to hire someone else?

At first, Beth didn't mind doing all of the housework, but it only took a few months for her to resent Jason for not doing his share. By the time they discussed the problem, Beth was so upset that it turned into a full-fledged argument that nearly split them apart. If they had decided ahead of time who would do what housework, the resentment and subsequent explosion might have been averted.

A 2016 study at the University of Michigan discovered that husbands create an extra seven hours per week of housework for most married women.[5] This means that married women without children do even more housework than single moms.[6] OMG! (The organization MenCare, which advocates for men to do an equal share of unpaid domestic labor, estimates that it will take at least seventy more years for married men in heterosexual couples to take over their full share of this work. OMG again!)

Dr. Darcy Lockman, author of *All the Rage: Mothers, Fathers, and the Myth of Equal Partnership*, wrote in the *New York Times* about a wife she interviewed who said her husband participated but couldn't be trusted to remember to do housework. Another wife said of her husband, "We fell into this easy pattern where he learned to be oblivious and I learned to resent him."[7] This is a tough one, and we don't have an easy solution. But when it comes to expectations about housework, just like any other expectations, the key is to communicate what you want and need.

**3.** *We expect we'll always feel as intensely in love as on the day of our wedding.* Wouldn't it be nice if we humans worked like that? Most people don't even like their spouse some days, let alone feel any love for them. This doesn't mean they've fallen *out* of love, but life brings ups and downs that cause our feelings to fluctuate wildly. Plus, there's a scientific reason for the rush we feel when we first fall in love. It's a literal rush in our body of feel-good chemicals like oxytocin and serotonin. Those high levels of chemicals have to come down eventually, leaving some people sure that something has gone wrong. But that isn't necessarily the case. It just means it's time to be a grown-up living in the real world rather than a prince and princess in a fantasy kingdom. Sigh. When the feel-good chemical levels return to normal, the quirk we used to think was cute may suddenly become an annoyance. If we know this is going to happen and *expect* it, that can help us handle it better without assuming our relationship is in trouble. The romantic love we feel at the beginning of a relationship is fantastic, but the deep love that can be built by two mature adults can be even better and even more romantic in a way that's profound and lasting.

4. *We assume the person we marry will stay the same person.* We all change and grow, and sometimes, we grow in different directions. If we maintain a high level of emotional intimacy from day to day, we can sometimes navigate these changes with minimal conflict. If we don't and just go through the motions without staying truly connected to each other, we might feel shocked and betrayed when our spouse appears to have changed overnight.

We knew a couple where both had a naïve expectation that the person they married would always stay the same, but the reality was the opposite. Rob and Megan had been married for eight years when Megan went through a spiritual awakening. She stopped drinking, started meditating, and got involved with Buddhist groups. It made her very happy and lowered her stress levels. But it was disconcerting for Rob. He was used to going to bars with his wife and doing most activities together. Plus, he wasn't interested in sharing her newfound spirituality. This caused problems in their marriage, and they worried it might break them up.

It took some couples counseling and lots of conversations to come to an understanding about the changes Megan had experienced. Eventually, however, Rob was able to accept the person she had become, and Megan was able to accept that Rob didn't want to join her Buddhist groups. They stayed together because they genuinely loved and trusted the core of the other person, and they made a conscious decision not to require each other to be anyone other than who they were.

Sometimes, though, we can't navigate these changes because they make us no longer compatible. What we have to remember is that such changes are inevitable, and all we can do is our best to work through them and maintain the love we have for each other.

5. *Some people expect the opposite—that once they get married, their partner will magically change into the person they want.* They figure all they need is time to mold their partner and get them into shape. Our desire to be in love can cause us to rush into marriage, especially if we feel pressured by parents, friends, and/or society. We might gloss over issues and assume everything will somehow work out. Unfortunately, that rarely happens. Expecting to change someone is a recipe for a failed marriage. It rarely works and can be a breeding ground for resentment.

6. *We expect that marriage will and should be easy.* Then, at the first sign of a conflict, we think we should split up. How many times do people say in movies, "I don't think this should be so hard." Who says? In her *New York Times* article, Dr. Darcy Lockman interviewed a man who said that, with the exception of honoring fidelity, most of his male friends expected married life to be the same as when they were single. In other words, they didn't expect it to be more work at all. Unfortunately, they had a rude awakening. A healthy marriage, just like a healthy body, is *work*. We have to be willing to talk through our issues and find ways to compromise with each other. If there's a lot of conflict or unspoken resentment, you can be sure some work is required. Without that work, issues fester and grow like weeds in an abandoned lot, and problems that were once small can become much bigger. We always suggest therapy because it helps so much to have a third, objective party to help couples come to a place of common ground.

7. *We put on our best behavior throughout our dating life because we expect we'd be rejected if we showed our true self.* Then, we try to keep up the façade once we're married, but it's like trying to carry a pile of bricks on our shoulders every day. There's simply no way to keep up the pretense. When we finally let it go, our spouse looks at us and says, "Who the hell are you?" They don't recognize us because we have been pretending to be someone else for as long as they've known us. Needless to say, this doesn't bode well. Our

partner feels betrayed and blindsided by this different person they suddenly see. Plus, if we pretend to be someone we are not, we never feel truly loved for who we are. Only in being transparent and authentic can we give someone else the opportunity to love us, as we give ourselves the chance to feel loved for our real self.

8. *We think our spouse is responsible for our happiness.* After all, doesn't every romantic movie seem to indicate that happiness is due to their true love? Don't get us wrong—a good marriage certainly has the potential to contribute to our happiness. But the reality is that if we don't find it within ourselves to create our own happiness and self-esteem, nobody else will be able to do it for us. It's the epitome of an inside job. Yet, if we don't feel happy most of the time once we get married, we assume something's wrong with our partner or the marriage rather than our own ability to create happiness. (We could write a whole chapter on unrealistic expectations about happiness and what's required to feel happy, but that's for another book!)

9. *We think our partner will never hurt us.* When you live with someone, it's inevitable that they'll do something that hurts you at some point, no matter how hard they might try not to. Life is messy, and we all trip up. We say things that aren't meant to hurt others, but they do anyway. We lose our temper and say things we don't mean. This is why forgiveness and understanding are necessities in any kind of relationship.

10. *We have different expectations about how much space and time we should have apart from each other.* One person in the relationship may think, "Once we get married, we'll spend all of our time together! Can't wait!" The other person might assume that they'll have alone time and might need some separate space at times to feel good about the relationship. For the person expecting to spend every moment together, it can feel like their partner doesn't love them as much, but that probably has nothing to do with it. This is simply a difference in personalities and, yes, expectations. You

can see how this could lead to a big blowout unless it's discussed beforehand or at least with an understanding that these differences don't necessarily mean one person loves the other more.

11. *We think our spouse is the only friend we need.* This puts a lot of pressure on the relationship and can feel smothering to the other person. Friendships with others, whether separately or as a couple, bring different perspectives and energy into the relationship. They provide a cushion when both people are going through something painful, and they can be a sounding board when there's a conflict in the marriage. They also allow us to pursue interests when our partner doesn't share them. One person might love to perform in community theater, while the other person is into golf. Plus, it's healthy at times for men to hang out with other men and for women to hang out with other women rather than always spending time in the company of men and women together.

12. *We expect our partner to be able to read our mind.* "Doesn't he know he should put the toilet seat down?" "Doesn't she know I don't want to always be the one to initiate sex?" If they aren't already doing it, they probably don't know. So we get upset and assume they just don't care. Nine times out of ten, they have no idea because we haven't bothered to say anything. It's silly when you think about this logically, yet almost all of us are guilty of this at some point in our lives. If you find yourself holding on to resentment toward your partner, ask yourself if you've actually communicated what you want from them.

13. *We expect our sex life will always be great because we love each other and had hot chemistry before marriage.* But keeping a long-term sex life steamy requires conscious work for most couples. It doesn't just take care of itself. We have to be willing to communicate with each other about what we want and need, as well as be willing to try new things to keep sex from becoming boring. Then, of course, there are the expectations about how much sex to have on a regular basis. It's different when people start living

together, so it's helpful to know how much each person likes to have sex regularly. One person may like it three times a week, while the other person may feel that once a week or less is fine. This issue might not come up during dating, so it can create a lot of resentment if it isn't discussed and resolved in some way before it becomes a problem.

14. *We expect our partner to finally heal us from feeling unloved.* While it may be a salve to feel loved by someone, we still have to do the work to heal our childhood trauma. If we don't feel lovable, no one else's love is going to fill that hole—not completely. Again, this is an inside job. This also means that as soon as our partner gets upset with us about anything, we feel shaky about our lovability, which can lead us to needy behavior. We might do whatever our partner wants in order to win their approval again, or we might beg them to stay with us, which can make our partner feel uncomfortable and burdened. So it's on each of us to work on our own healing through reading books like this and through therapy. We can learn how to love ourselves so that we don't expect our partner to make sure we feel lovable enough. When we do that, the love we receive from them is wonderful but not something we need in order to feel okay about who we are.

15. *We expect that our spouse will be fine with our parents and extended family meddling in our relationship.* Not all family systems operate like that, and our spouse may not be fine with it at all. It may be foreign to them and feel too enmeshed and intrusive. If your family thinks they'll have a say in your relationship or how you raise your kids, your partner might (probably will) consider it a major boundary violation. Even if you're fine with meddling parents and siblings, we recommend discussing it with both your spouse and your family. Everyone's expectations need to be addressed before a situation arises and detonates like dynamite, and everyone needs to know where the boundary lines have been drawn. If they don't like it, you might have to get tough because your marriage just may depend on it.

**16.** *We have negative expectations that give our partner a pass.* Women might think "boys will be boys" and expect a husband to cheat, while a man involved with a woman he sees as particularly beautiful might assume she will cheat on him. These expectations that we will be disappointed might stem from what happened to us in previous relationships or what we observed in adult relationships during our childhood. Rather than expecting too much of our partner, we might expect too little. This can set us up for feeling paranoid about what our spouse might do or even accepting abusive behavior from our partner because we either expect it as normal or we think we don't deserve better. Again, awareness is key here. When we realize we're doing this, we can recognize it as unhealthy and make a conscious effort to stop expecting too little or the worst. It isn't something anyone can just stop on a dime, but with awareness, we can gradually change our thinking and expectations to be more self-loving.

**17.** *In same-sex relationships, the two people might assume they are automatically on the same page.* But people are different even if they identify similarly. Just because two partners are gay, for example, doesn't mean they don't have different expectations based on their upbringing, community, and experiences. People who are non-cisgender or in non-heterosexual relationships need to have those same important conversations.

Hey, we know it's scary to speak up about issues with the people we love because we worry we'll end up starting an argument. But not speaking up is much more likely to cause an argument, especially when we sweep issues under the rug and harbor resentment. When we have the courage to discuss differences and issues before bad feelings escalate, we have a much better chance of maintaining a good relationship.

# FUCKING THE EXPECTATIONS DOESN'T MEAN WE DON'T COMPROMISE

Just because you are fucking the expectations doesn't mean you get to be an ass to everyone around you! None of us would be able to get along with anyone without some healthy compromise in the mix. The trick is figuring out if you're compromising enough or too much. If you're the one always making concessions, that's a problem. But if you're the one who *never* makes concessions, that's also a problem. We all have to weigh our own desires against what others need and want. It's always important to be considerate and caring.

What if the compromise you're being asked to make isn't about whether to see the rom-com versus the action flick but about some regular behavior on your part? In our experience, you have to ask yourself if you'd be compromising who you are or just softening your edges. Most of us have a few rough edges that could use a little smoothing. For example, your partner might tell you that your particular brand of sarcastic humor feels hurtful to them at times. While you might like this aspect of your personality, you don't want your partner to feel hurt. You decide to be more careful and sensitive when using sarcasm. Here's another example: your spouse is very affectionate and expects to hear "I love you" every day. This is uncomfortable for you because your family was never expressive in this way. But you want to do this for your spouse, so you agree to move beyond your comfort zone and learn how to be more affectionate.

On the other hand, it's almost certainly too much to ask if your spouse expects you to spend 100 percent of your time with them and have no contact with others or if you're expected to accept abusive behavior from your spouse's relatives. Only you can decide what's agreeable to you and what's too much of a compromise.

It's definitely a balancing act, but if you lead with love for both your partner and yourself and avoid blaming the other person, you have a good chance of reaching an agreement, especially if you work on your communication skills. And as we've said several times already, therapy is the best method we have found for breaking a stalemate!

If you're married, engaged, or thinking about it, consider your expectations, check the unreasonable ones at the door, and talk them out with your other half. Again, from what we've seen, that's the best way to ensure your marriage is solid and lasting.

## EXPECTATION: YOU SAY NO NOW, BUT YOU WILL WANT KIDS EVENTUALLY

This is what many people are told by family and friends when they dare to say they don't want to have children. The pressure is real, people!

Almost half of US women between the ages of twenty-five and thirty-four have said they feel pressured to have kids.[8] The strong implication is that motherhood is a female's biological destiny, and that every single woman in the world has maternal instincts. We don't assume all men have paternal instincts, though, do we?

In 2015, Pope Francis went so far as to say, "The choice to not have children is selfish."[9] (Yes, he really said this!) The Catholic Church also still prohibits birth control beyond the rhythm method—based on predicting when a woman might get pregnant depending on where she is in her menstrual cycle (good luck with that). In America at least, women are apparently giving the middle finger to this idea that not having children is selfish because nearly half of us are child-free (the now-preferred term over "child*less*").[10]

It seems these adults have asked the same questions we want to ask: Is it selfish to live the one life you have on your own terms, or is it selfish to bring children into the world when your heart isn't in it? Who is hurt if we choose not to have children? It's no question that children are hurt every day by parents who don't really want them or know how to properly care for them.

For instance, our societal expectations of mothers are a big problem. Most mothers who are depressed after giving birth only feel more depressed a year on.[11] Can you say *burnout*? It's true that more men seem to be stepping up to take care of kids.[12] But you'll also find articles by mothers who bemoan society's tendency to applaud fathers for changing one diaper or spending one afternoon with the kids, as if that's equivalent to what the mother is doing, which is simply viewed as her *job*.

Another expectation that many people seem to have is that we should feel comfortable talking about our parental status with strangers. Some might casually ask: *Why don't you have kids? Didn't you want to have kids? Did you try to have kids?* Yet aren't these loaded and intrusive questions? Those who didn't want to have children don't want to answer because they're too often criticized for their decision. Those who have lost a child or were never able to conceive, perhaps even spending years and a lot of money trying fertility treatments to no avail, don't want to tell an acquaintance about something so personal and painful. (Privacy, please.)

Our friend Bridgett told us that within two months after she gave birth to her first child, her family started pressuring her to have another. "My aunt told me it would be abusive to our baby to not give her a brother or sister," Bridgett says. "I was stunned. I mean, *dramatic much*? I was even more stunned that my mother nodded her head in agreement. I didn't know what to say in the moment because they caught me off guard. But when the subject came up again, I told them both it was my decision to make with my husband. When my aunt brought it up yet again, I told her in no uncertain terms that it was not up for discussion. She acted hurt about it for a while but eventually got over it."

It turns out that psychologists in the 1800s came up with the idea of only child syndrome, claiming that only children were lonely, spoiled, less social, and not as well-adjusted as children with siblings. A lot of people still believe these theories even though they have long since been debunked. Today's more in-the-know psychologists agree that only children are just as well-adjusted as kids with brothers and sisters.[13]

When people genuinely want children, it's a beautiful thing. Keri is the first to say, "My son is someone I love beyond anything else in the world. It's a profound love." The problem is when we give in to the expectation of our family, friends, or society to have children without ever questioning it. It's easy to fall prey to these expectations because who wants to be judged or criticized for remaining child-free? Who wants pressure from their parents to give them grandchildren? (Parents can wish for grandchildren and feel disappointed if they don't get them, but the last thing they should ever do is pressure their children to procreate.)

Whether child-*full* or child-*free*, the key to happiness, in our opinion, is choosing based on what you truly want. If you don't yet have children, have you thought about whether you *really* want them and why, or have you agreed because of your spouse, family, or religion? You owe it to yourself, your partner, and your potential children to think this through.

## Ask Yourself: Marriage and Children Expectations

Take a look at the box you created at the end of chapter 1 for love/marriage. How small was it? After reading this chapter, do you need to adjust it to a different size?

If you're married, do you feel pressured to have children or to have more children if you already have some? If you're single, do you feel pressured to get married and have children? If so, where does that pressure come from? Parents? Spouse? Extended family? Peers? Culture? Your own fears or beliefs about how your life should be?

If you haven't followed the expectations of others to marry or have children, have you felt guilty about it?

Have you resented the pressure you have received, and have you pushed back with anyone who has tried to convince you of what you *should* do?

If you're receiving pressure now, what would you like to say to the people who are putting that expectation on you?

If you're married, did you have the wedding you wanted or the one your parents, spouse, or in-laws wanted? If you're planning a wedding, which traditions do you like, and which do you dislike? If you were to go against tradition, would anyone in your circle be upset with you? If so, how would you handle it?

Do you have expectations about what your relationship or parental status should be that haven't been fulfilled? Can you ease those expectations of yourself while still working toward what you want?

Chances are, at some point in your life, unspoken expectations have caused an argument between you and a romantic partner. Look back on those times and be honest with yourself about what happened. If you're currently in a relationship, what expectations on both sides are causing friction? What can you discuss with your partner to get clearer about these expectations and reach a compromise?

When you have unearthed some of the marriage and children expectations that may have held you back, write down the one that you feel has been the most influential and consequential in your life.

What do you feel are the consequences of holding on to this expectation for the rest of your life?

If you weren't afraid of the consequences, would you immediately let go of this expectation? If you did, how would your life look?

## THE INEVITABLE OVERLAP

Now, if you compare your notes from this and the previous chapters, there's a good chance you'll have some crossover expectations. For example, one of the expectations many women face that might not suit them is that they will work in jobs that have been traditionally female. That one often comes from several directions: family, religion, gender, and culture. It's a four-headed dragon that is definitely slayable, but it might take some extra effort. While you can follow the same plan for nixing expectations that come from multiple places, it helps to know exactly where and with whom you might have to push back to keep each expectation at bay.

# CHAPTER 7
# Nice to Meet You! What Do You Do?

Over the course of the average life, we spend about 90,000 hours at work.[1] Doesn't that statistic make you want to take a nap? *On a beach?*

That's a lot of hours to be miserable if you hate your job or career. It's a lot of hours to feel stuck in the wrong profession. But how many of us do that? And how many of us do it because of an expectation that has been placed on us by either our own thinking or someone else's? If our podcast guests are any indication, a lot of people hate their jobs. So many of our guests have told us about how they got trapped in a career they couldn't stand. But they each found a way out of that particular box and into a career where they could be happy and thrive.

There is no firm data on how many people change careers over their lifetime, but estimates are that the average person changes careers three to seven times over the course of their life.[2] This makes sense to us because no one is the same person they were ten years ago, let alone twenty or more years ago. It's crazy that we are often expected to know at age sixteen or seventeen what we want to do for the rest of our life. It might feel like a tremendous waste if our parents spent thousands of dollars on years of law school, medical school, or the like. But doesn't it sound like an even worse waste to spend *90,000* hours over the course of a life doing something you dislike?

—

In this chapter, we will ask you to examine the expectations that might have kept you stuck in a career or job that doesn't make you happy. Let's look at some of the common expectations that might squeeze you into a box. But first, let's talk about where those expectations might come from.

## CAREER EXPECTATIONS CAN COME FROM ALL DIRECTIONS

Our expectations with regard to career usually come from family, religion, or culture. Our parents are often the first ones to put the pressure on. After all, they're the people who usually foot the bill for college or maybe have a legacy business that they want desperately to keep in the family (i.e., with you). Or they are afraid you'll take up a profession that's too risky or doesn't pay well enough to keep you flush with cash (and out of their basement).

Our podcast guest Eileen Tarjan followed in her parents' footsteps into the corporate world, taking a position at a public relations agency. She felt stuck there for more than a decade until she was finally let go while the agency went through a not-so-agreeable merger. As she was packing up her office, someone asked her, "Are you going to do your own thing now?"

Eileen thought, *Well, that's an idea!* She wasn't yet sure what her *own thing* might be, but she was ready to get out of her stifling career box. Even though she went from a six-figure income to zero in one fell swoop, she slept well that night. She was lucky in that she had a financial cushion, so she resisted the urge to look for another corporate position. Instead, she says, "I sat my ass down quietly and figured it out."

While changing professions doesn't always mean you have to go back to school, Eileen opted to get a master's degree in clinical mental health counseling. Now she has a career as a life coach that gives her a strong sense of purpose.

Culture might also put expectations on us that can get in the way of our career choices. In some communities, for example, it's expected that everyone will go to college, while in others, it's expected that *no one* will. Or we might be expected to only go into certain professions because it's what most everyone else where we live has done.

Certainly, gender can cause us to brush off professions that we might be interested in if they weren't considered by society to be only for men or only for women. Our friend Ken went through this when he decided to pursue nursing. His friends made fun of him relentlessly, and it got bad enough that he almost gave up the idea. But he persevered and found that he loved his work.

Wherever the expectations come from, they can put us in a pretty miniscule box that prevents us from pursuing the career or job we truly want or even figuring out what we might enjoy if we didn't feel restricted.

## EXPECTATION: YOU CAN'T MAKE MONEY DOING WHAT YOU LOVE

We once knew a man named Vince who had wanted to become a philosophy professor, but his father told him, "You can't make money as a philosopher!" So he took a job as an IT consultant, and every day was soul-crushing (that's the tightest kind of box there is). It took him years, but eventually, he finished his degree in philosophy and realized his dream. Shifting gears wasn't easy for him by any stretch, but he was so much happier. "I have deep discussions with colleagues and students about what it means to be human," he told us, by then in his thirties. "It fulfills a very profound need in me, while working in IT felt robotic. Most of my colleagues there loved it, but it was 100 percent wrong for my personality."

Our podcast guest Robert Markowitz started out as a criminal lawyer to please his parents. Even though he was an artistic type, he admits he wasn't brave, so he took the safe road. When people asked him what he was going to do after earning his undergraduate degree, he discovered that saying "Duke Law" impressed them enough to shut them up. No more questions meant no judgments.

"I knew deep down that it [the law] wasn't really for me, but I was willing to try to fake it until I made it," Robert says. He practiced law for about four years until he began to lose his ability to feel. "I would go to movies just to be able to cry because otherwise, I didn't feel anything . . . I was operating in that one square inch of logical brain matter all the time."

Then he started doing volunteer childcare at a church. "A girl was playing duck, duck, goose, and she slipped and cut herself. And for some reason, she leapt into my arms crying," Robert says. "I had this moment where I was like, 'Wow, there is more to life than the little square that I've been trapped in for years now.' It just really affected me."

He started looking at the employment ads, but most of them were for jobs he wasn't interested in. Then he saw an ad that promised to train him in one evening to be a party clown. They would send him out to birthday parties in New York City and pay him almost nothing. But Robert immediately thought, "That's what I want!" Something stirred inside him, making him feel less dead inside. At his first party performing as "Bobo the Clown," a seven-year-old boy said, "Bobo, I love you!"

Robert went back to his car and leaned his head against the steering wheel. "I was like, 'Oh, man, what is that feeling? I forgot about this feeling. What do they call that feeling? Oh . . . happiness?'" It didn't happen overnight, but eventually, Pottery Barn Kids hired him to travel up and down the East Coast to perform at their stores, for which he was paid about ten times his original fee as a clown.

He was able to find a way to make a living doing what he loved in an unconventional profession. Bravo, Robert!

## EXPECTATION: IT'S A GOOD JOB—WHY CHANGE?

If you're making lots of money or have plenty of prestige, and your job is going well, people might look at you as though you have two heads if you want to change. That is a tough decision to make—even if you're miserable. There are successful actors who give it up for a quieter life, and people just assume they can't get work. Who says we have to stay in a job we hate just because it's considered safe and stable by others? Who says we have to stay in a career even if we spent time and money on the education for it? If we hate every minute of it, why are we there?

Heck, people will tell you not to leave a job that may not be remotely safe or stable, just because there's a chance you'll find it hard to get another. Yes, it can be scary, and we would never suggest that anyone leave a job they need to support themselves without a safety net. But remember how many hours you spend at work. Don't you owe yourself the chance of finding a job that you can truly enjoy? It might take time, but even if financial restraints mean you need to stay in a job you hate, don't assume you will have to stay there forever. Begin to evaluate your options. Talk to other people, do research whenever you have a free moment, and open your mind to the possibility that there's something else you could do that would actually be fun. Sometimes, a big part of making that kind of change is believing you can do it.

Our podcast guest Nadine Chapman wasn't even miserable in her job. She just wanted more. And why shouldn't she try to have it?

Nadine was a lawyer for the federal government, and she was quickly promoted through the ranks to the highest position she could get there. But she started to feel unsettled. One day, her inner voice said, "You are so much bigger than this right now. You need to play in a larger sandbox." She wasn't unhappy, but she didn't feel she was growing enough. "I was ready to fly, but the environment that I was in was not giving me that perch I needed to lift off from," she says.

That's when an old dream resurfaced. Her great-aunt had worked at the World Bank and regaled Nadine with fascinating stories about it. Whenever one of her aunt's colleagues traveled to a new country, they would bring back a doll for Nadine. Her collection of dolls from all over the world reached thirty-five in total. She asked someone who worked there what it would take for her to get a job with the organization. "You're not an economist; you don't speak multiple languages. The likelihood of you getting into the World Bank is not great," they told her.

Well . . . that was hard to hear. Plus, when her mother found out about her decision to leave "the good government job," she didn't exactly approve. She expected Nadine to stay in that comfy job and thought it was bonkers to start over. That disapproval wasn't easy to swallow because Nadine and her mother are extremely close.

But Nadine describes herself as hardheaded. "You're not going to stop me from my aspiration." Nevertheless, it was daunting. "It was going into foreign territory. I would have to literally start all over again at a point in my life where I could have easily coasted in my boat on the ocean," she says.

Still, she was ready. "I had a clear vision, and I had a goal. And that goal was in alignment with my values and where I saw myself going," she says. She leveraged her strengths and was able to secure a starting position as a mediation officer with a small team at her dream employer, the World Bank. She admits the transition wasn't always easy. The environment and culture were completely different from what she was used to, and it took her a couple of years to completely adjust. However, looking back on it more than twenty years later and after being promoted, she says, "It was one of the best decisions I have made in my life." Today, she is the World Bank's Manager of Mediation Services.

Nadine emphasizes that each of us is unique, and we have at least one strength or talent that we can use to help us make a change. The question is whether we have identified that strength or talent and whether we are leveraging it to our advantage. "My ingredient has been my communication and conflict-resolution skills," she told us. She has found a way to mix that ingredient into every job she has ever had. She's quite the inspiration.

Nadine is a great example of how incredibly important it is to get to know yourself well enough to discover what will make you happy. If you're leaving a good job for your dream, it's a leap of faith, but we believe you owe yourself that leap. You might have to live on a reduced income, and some of your loved ones might disapprove. But your emotional and physical well-being matter most.

## SUBTLE, HARD-TO-RECOGNIZE EXPECTATIONS

Some expectations come from within us. In the words of an old horror movie, *the call is coming from inside the house.* They can be much more difficult to pinpoint. Might that be the case for you? See if the stories and scenarios on the next few pages give you a new perspective on your own situation.

Often, for example, we aren't even fully aware that we're dissatisfied at work because we've become so single-minded about reaching the goal we set for ourselves. We don't stop to think if that goal suits the person we have become.

That's what happened to our lawyer friend, Cliff, who had been an associate with a large corporate firm where the partner track generally took eight years. When nine years came and went, he realized he was never going to make partner in the firm. "It was a blow, but it jarred me awake," he says. "I finally stopped to think, 'Wait a minute. Do I really want this?'" He had been concentrating on making partner for so long that he never stopped to ask himself if he actually liked what he was doing (sometimes for sixty hours a week). He had put off dating and marriage in the pursuit of this carrot that he thought he was *supposed* to want. It was a self-expectation that no longer served who he was or what he genuinely desired.

"I loved the law, so I didn't want to leave the profession entirely," he says. "But I also wanted to do something that held more meaning for me. I fell in love with the law because I wanted to help people, not big corporations like I had ended up doing." Eventually, Cliff found a position as an in-house lawyer for a nonprofit organization. He loved it. "Did I take a pay cut?" he says. "Sure. But I didn't mind it because for the first time in a while, I didn't struggle to get up in the morning. I looked forward to going to work." He also went back to a normal forty-hour workweek and found time to date again.

What expectation might you be holding over your own head, preventing you from spending your 90,000 allotted work hours doing something you actually enjoy? Let's look at the most common ones:

1. *You expected to retire in your current job, so leaving it seems unthinkable.* That's what Tom Glaser expected—a topic he discussed on our podcast. He was in his dream job in the counseling department of a college, providing individual psychotherapy. "I was determined my plan was to retire there," he says. Then, after seven years, something changed. A coworker was hired who hated Tom and undermined him at every turn. Tom tried everything he could think of to rectify the problem, but nothing worked. He became very depressed until his husband said, "You can't do this anymore." Tom said he needed that mirror to make him come to terms with the fact that his plan wasn't going to pan out.

"I think the universe was saying, 'Hey, there's other stuff you can do,'" he says. Even though he admits it was a huge risk, especially because he didn't have a Plan B, he quit the job. He went into private practice and wrote the Amazon best-selling book, *Full Heart Living: Conversations with the Happiest People I Know*. While he admits he still misses aspects of the job he left, he has no regrets.

2.    *You feel you can't leave your current career because you have no idea what else you would do.* But as Eileen Tarjan did, when she left the corporate world to become a career and life coach/psychotherapist, we might have to "sit our ass down" to figure things out. In this case, we think you're expecting too little of yourself. You just might have to do some investigating and research. We're going to talk more about this in chapter 9, but don't let yourself stay stuck for years just because the alternative hasn't come to you yet. If you look for it, it will!

3.    *You believe you're too old to do something different.* This is another case where your expectation of yourself is too small. If you have to learn an entirely new field, we get that it can feel daunting when you're in midlife. But lots of people have done it . . . and successfully. There is no reason why you can't start over if that's what you want. You might have to take a deep breath and trust yourself in spite of your fears, but it's worth it.

4.    *You worry that financially, you wouldn't be able to handle a career or job switch.* That's certainly a valid fear, but we also know many people who have found a way. We don't believe it makes sense to be defeatist about it and convince yourself that you have no alternative. Again, we think you're selling yourself short by automatically expecting that you can't do it. No matter how impossible it may seem, we urge you to look for possibilities and surprising opportunities so that you don't miss them when they show up. Yes, it might take some time and ingenuity, but if you're determined, we believe you can figure out how to make the change without losing your shirt.

5. *You think you'll have to take a pay cut and give up your lifestyle.*
This is a real issue that you will have to think about. It could be
that the new profession you would like to try pays considerably
less than what you do now. If that's true, you will have to decide
which is more important to you: your lifestyle or the way you feel
during your hours at work. Only you can know; there is no right or
wrong answer. But it's an important decision to make.

We don't want to minimize how scary this can be. But as Liz
Alterman told us on our podcast, "I think when you're stuck, you
have this fear within you . . . that you're going to make a wrong
decision. Sometimes, it's better to make a decision, and then you
can course-correct as opposed to just standing still and doing
nothing." We are often so afraid of regret that we convince ourselves it's easier to live with a struggle. It's that old saying about
being less afraid of the devil you know versus the devil you don't
know. But talk about a suffocating box!

## THIS JOB IS COSTING ME MY HEALTH!

You've already read about Robert Markowitz and Tom Glaser, who
were truly suffering in their jobs. If they had forced themselves to
stay, who knows what might have happened to their health. (We
hate to think!) Our podcast guest Andy Lee waited until it was
almost too late.

Andy was working for Merrill Lynch. For a long time, he felt the
need building in him to leave that job, but he describes himself as
having been "pretty deep in denial."

"I was basically kind of checked out in my life and just putting
one step, one foot in front of the other," he says. "Pretending everything's fine, when my body certainly knew that everything wasn't
fine, and my mental state was telling me everything wasn't fine."

Then, one day, he just couldn't bear to go into work. Despite all the warning signs from his body, the reality that he couldn't continue that job for another minute hit him like a bolt of lightning and shook him out of his stupor.

According to Andy, that kind of denial was rampant in his profession. "I definitely saw it on Wall Street in the financial sector, certainly where people get blinders on in certain careers," he says. He told us that plenty of his colleagues had decided they knew what it would take to be successful, and they didn't care what it cost them. But that single-mindedness can lead to unhealthy outcomes. He suggests that we all stop long enough to ask ourselves: *Just because everyone tells me this is what I need to do, and even though it's what I've told myself I've wanted for twenty years, is it really what I want now? Do I still want to do this?*

Andy ended up getting treated for depression to get himself healthy. He began to learn mindfulness meditation for his own well-being, and before he knew it, that's what became his profession. (We love this so much!) "Teaching it has helped me to stay on track personally, and it's just so rewarding . . . It's really changed my perspective on things," he says. Eventually, he became Chief Mindfulness Officer for Aetna Insurance (yes, *that* Aetna) and later founded his own company called Mindful Ethos. Again, Andy proves that you *can* make a living doing what you love. You don't have to stay in a job that's hurting your health.

## YOUR JOB DOESN'T DEFINE YOU

All too often, we think our profession defines who we are. Americans might even be more prone to identification via career than people in other parts of the world. Back to cultural expectations!

We seem to have a particular work ethic in this country that dates back to before the country was founded (from the 1600s when the Pilgrims arrived on the *Mayflower*). According to a 2022 CNBC article, "'Work is the most important way of proving your worth,' and it's making Americans miserable."

If our worth is tied up with our work, what does that do to us when we lose our job? Nothing good. It can cause intense anxiety and shame or send us into a terrible depression.

In the article, Ofer Sharone, professor of sociology at the University Massachusetts Amherst, said that when we're unemployed for a long time, people in some cultures might blame the system, while we Americans are more likely to blame ourselves.

Obviously, work is important for us to survive, but striving for status can keep us in a box that says work = worth, and worth = work. That same article contends that people in countries where they focus more on leisure time find it easier to stay happy even if they suffer a job loss.[3] That makes sense because when we put so much emphasis on work, our lives can end up feeling hollow.

That's the way it was for Helen, a woman we met through a mutual friend. "I was always very much a feminist, so I'd wanted to be a career woman for as long as I can remember," she says. "Even when I was a toddler, I looked up to all the businesswomen I saw on TV. I pictured myself in one of those suits and wearing power pumps. That's who I wanted to be, so I made sure it happened for me as an adult. For a long time, I was happy, but I started to burn out because my whole life was my work. I didn't have any friends who weren't at the office, and I couldn't really call them friends because there was too much backstabbing and competition. I didn't date because I wanted to focus on my career. I had no hobbies and no community outside of my company, and it started to weigh on me."

Then, the unimaginable happened. Helen's company folded when the founder died. Suddenly, she was without a job, and her sense of identity was without an anchor.

"I was given a severance package," she says, "so I decided to use it to find out who I was outside of this job that had supposedly created me. I began to do volunteer work and developed relationships outside of my company that were *true* friendships. I also discovered a love of nature photography that gave me a sense of identity beyond work."

When Helen went back into the workforce a few months later, she found a company with a more relaxed culture. She no longer wanted to work long hours or put everything she had into her career. While she wanted to remain single, she also wanted a more balanced and well-rounded life that allowed her to define herself as a good friend, a community activist, a nature enthusiast, and an artist. She finally realized that her career was just *one* aspect of her life, not its totality.

Now that you've read about some of the common expectations that can keep us boxed in with regard to career, what have you discovered about yourself? Let's ask some of those important questions to figure out what adjustments you might need to make in this aspect of your life.

## Ask Yourself: Career Expectations

Take a look at the box you created at the end of chapter 1 for career and work. Do you need to adjust it to be smaller or larger?

Did you choose your current profession because you loved it or because someone else told you it was what you *should* do? Were you pressured by your family, religion, culture, or gender expectations to choose your career? If so, which ones affected you the most—family, religion, culture, or gender? What did people say to you that made you feel you had to choose that career? Would you have chosen a different profession or job if you didn't have to worry about any of these expectations?

Have you thought about changing your career or job? What have you thought about doing instead? What is scariest about making that change, and what do you worry would happen? Would people in your life judge you if you switched?

If you want to start your own business, is there a way you could do it as a side hustle until it works for you full time? That's what Dr. Denise Moore Revel has done. When we spoke to her on our podcast, she told us about transitioning from her work as a speech pathologist to her work as a coach in her Own Your Amazing coaching practice. While it has been challenging to do both, it has kept her financially flush while she builds her practice and works toward doing it full time.

When you have unearthed some of the career expectations that may have held you back, write down the one that has been the most influential and consequential in your life. Which one is boxing you in the most, whether it is inflicted on you by other people or your own expectations of yourself?

What do you feel are the consequences of continuing this expectation for the rest of your life? What within yourself would you have to sacrifice, and is that sacrifice worth it? If you weren't afraid of the consequences, would you immediately let go of this career expectation? Would you go for a new job or career entirely? How would your life be different?

Here are some more questions that are helpful to ask yourself about career: How do you define success? Are you expressing who you are in your current job? When you lose yourself in your work and feel that you are in a state of flow, what tasks are you performing? When was the last time you felt proud at work, and what was the pride about? What do you want to feel most of the time while at work? What skills, talents, and experience do you have that might transfer to a different job or career?

# Part II

# Explore, Take Action, and Keep It Going!

# CHAPTER 8
# What the Hell Do You Really Want?

 Before you run off, sword brandished, ready to vanquish all manner of expectations, STOP! We're going to ask you to spend just a little bit more time on growing your awareness.

We want to help you figure out which expectations you want to vanquish first as well as what you might want *instead*. Again, you might find that in some areas of your life, you now know what you *don't* want, but you aren't sure what you *do* want. This next step, which is the third letter in BREAK, stands for *explore your possibilities*.

For instance, if you've spent your adult life adhering to the expectation that you would someday become a vice president of your company, only to realize that it isn't going to make you happy, it helps a hell of a lot to know what you want *instead*. If you're sitting there thinking, *I have no idea*, this part of the process will help.

First up on our agenda is learning more about your core values.

## HEY, YOU! WHAT DO YOU THINK IS MOST IMPORTANT?

Why do your values matter anyway? Well, they are like your own personal GPS. They drive your behavior. If you don't know what they are, it's like wandering through life with no map, going in circles or making turns into dead ends. Without making a conscious assessment of your values, your choices are more likely to be based on fleeting feelings and impressions than on what's meaningful to you.

In just a moment, we'll ask you to choose the values that mean the most to you. But what does this have to do with expectations? Let's say you choose Health as one of your core values. Yet, you've been holding on to an expectation that says you have to work at least sixty hours a week. In the meantime, you're exhausted, sleep-deprived, and rarely have time to exercise. Hmmm . . . that's a problem, isn't it? You'll need to let go of the expectation of working sixty hours every week if you want to honor your core value of Health. Knowing your values can (1) help you see which expectations might not be in alignment with what's most important to you, (2) help you better understand which ones need to be sent on their way sooner rather than later, and (3) figure out what the hell you actually want in life.

If you're letting go of expectations that mean a big change in your life like getting a divorce, letting go of a profession, switching religions, or having a huge boundary-setting conversation with your parents, your values will help you decide how to handle each of these situations. They will guide you to figure out what you want instead of these boxes you have been stuck inside (for who knows how long).

In short, values can not only help you step out of the box easier and faster, but they can help you know which direction you want to go once you've knocked those walls down. *In our experience, if you don't know yourself and your own core values, you're much more likely to be swayed by someone else's expectations. Conversely, when the weight of expectations is heavy on your back, it's much harder to live by your core values.* They are your filter for decision-making. They are your North Star.

You might be saying, "I've done these core values exercises before." If so, wonderful. You already have an idea of how they work. Still, we encourage you to do our version here as well. After all, our values shift and change throughout our lives. The answers you gave in the past may not be the same as your answers now. In fact, we do an exercise like this every year to see what might have changed and to keep our values at the forefront of our minds. And whenever you have to make a big decision, it can't hurt to have them handy to review again.

What's an example of a core value in action? When the two of us left the corporate world, we also took a financial hit. Our core values of Flexibility, Passion, and Mental Health took precedence over money, and we started our own business. For someone else, Money might be a core value that means they want to stay in a high-paying job. Another person might not care as much about money, but since Comfort and Stability are among their core values, they would probably never start their own business. It's all a matter of personal preference.

The two of us also share the core values of Empathy and Equality, so they drive our actions and decisions. For example, when Kelly was in high school, a teacher told her that some people just aren't meant for college, which was designed to discourage her from thinking about it. At first, hearing this from an adult made her feel worthless and hopeless. But now, Kelly has a master's degree, so that teacher was full of crap! Kelly chose to use that discouraging comment as fuel, and that has made her hell-bent on preventing anyone in her sphere from ever feeling like that teacher made her feel. It's especially important to her that people feel heard, accepted, and validated.

Authenticity is also a huge core value for both of us (no surprise). We facilitate Human Resources development calls with groups of HR pros, and they have told us they look forward to the calls because there's no façade, bullshit, or nonsense. It's a relief for them to be able to talk candidly without pretense. Keri in particular takes this as a badge of honor because her family thrived on maintaining that façade.

It's important to acknowledge here, too, that our values are examples of expectations that we *want* to have. We want to expect good things of ourselves (as long as, again, perfectionism doesn't get into the act). Remember that while we have spent most of our time talking about unwanted expectations, we all have wanted ones as well. And while examining our core values helps us determine which unwanted expectations to push out the window, it also helps us know which ones we want to invite in.

Below is a list of words that represent different values. Take a look at these and narrow them down to maybe the top ten that are most important to you. Make a separate list. If there is a value important to you that isn't on our list, feel free to add it to yours.

| | | | |
|---|---|---|---|
| Achievement | Adventure | Ambition | Animals |
| Appreciation | Art | Attractiveness | Authenticity |
| Authority | Autonomy | Balance | Beauty |
| Benevolence | Boldness | Brilliance | Calmness |
| Caring | Challenge | Charity | Cheerfulness |
| Cleanliness | Cleverness | Collaboration | Comfort |
| Commitment | Community | Compassion | Consistency |
| Contribution | Courage | Creativity and Imagination | Curiosity |
| Daring | Decisiveness | Dependability | Determination |
| Diversity | Emotions | Empathy | Encouragement |
| Enthusiasm | Equality | Ethics | Excellence |
| Excitement | Expertise | Expressiveness | Fairness and Justice |
| Faith | Family | Flexibility | Forgiveness |
| Freedom | Fun | Generosity | Gratitude |
| Growth | Happiness | Health | Helpfulness |
| Honesty | Humility | Humor | Inclusiveness |
| Independence | Individuality | Innovation | Inspiration |

| | | | |
|---|---|---|---|
| Integrity | Intelligence | Intuition | Joy |
| Kindness | Knowledge | Leadership | Learning |
| Leisure | Love | Loyalty | Mindfulness |
| Morality | Motivation | Nature | Open-Mindedness |
| Optimism | Originality | Passion | Patriotism |
| Peace | Performance | Persistence | Personal Development |
| Play and Playfulness | Pleasure | Popularity | Positivity |
| Power | Precision | Professionalism | Punctuality |
| Quality | Recognition | Relationships | Reliability |
| Resilience | Resourcefulness | Responsibility | Safety |
| Security | Self-Care | Self-Control | Selflessness |
| Self-Love | Self-Respect | Sensuality | Service |
| Simplicity | Spirituality | Stability | Style |
| Success | Tolerance | Traditionalism | Trust |
| Understanding | Uniqueness | Variety | Versatility |
| Vision | Warmth | Wealth | Wisdom |

If you included values that are similar, group them together. For example, you might link Honesty, Integrity, and Trust in one group. Putting them together in this way will help you narrow down your full list further to your top five core values. We know it's hard to eliminate so many, but it isn't like these top five are your *only* values; they are just the ones you believe matter to you the most right now.

Sam Thiara, founder of Ignite the Dream Coaching and Consulting, told us on our podcast about another way to think about these top five values: they are the five things you are most unwilling to compromise in your current life. It can be difficult to decide on what's more important than something else, but just do the best you can. Remember that you can change them as your awareness deepens.

Also bear in mind that these numbers are totally arbitrary. If you want to skip the longer list and jump to your top five, or if you want to start with a longer list than five, go ahead. We're just trying to give you a system to think about what you want to prioritize, but this is a book about doing whatever the hell you want. Please do what works for you!

And hey, if you want to keep your five values top of mind, you might take a cue from our podcast guest Scott Jeffrey Miller, who hosts his own podcast, *On Leadership with Scott Miller*. He chose seven values instead of five and created an acronym using the first letter of each—PHILPA, which stands for Purpose, Health, Integrity, Loyalty, Positivity, Abundance, and Learning. We thought that was a cool idea!

## DO YOU LIVE YOUR VALUES?

It's one thing to declare what you value most, but do you live your life based on those values? Remember our earlier example about the person who valued health but then realized they were working themselves into the ground. That kind of thing can happen to the best of us! In fact, it happens so often that psychologists have given it a name: the "value-action gap."[1]

For happiness expert/psychology professor Dr. Kennon Sheldon, who wrote a book called *Freely Determined: What the New Psychology of the Self Teaches Us About How to Live*, it's a kind of discordance. He talks about how we want the opposite of that—*self-concordance*, which means we act in a way that's consistent with our values. In other words, we're authentic. We don't abide by expectations or act in ways that are out of alignment with our values. If we live by someone else's expectations rather than our own, we are no doubt being inauthentic, or discordant with our values.[2] And Dr. Sheldon's research shows that authenticity and self-concordance make us happier, less anxious, and less depressed.[3] Isn't letting go of expectations, breaking out of the box, and doing whatever the hell we want all about being happier, less anxious, and less depressed? Hell, yeah!

Let's say Freedom is a core value for you, but the expectations of your family and church have made you feel anything but free. They expect you to follow strict rules of behavior. As a result, you are discordant, or out of alignment, with this value. If you want to honor Freedom, you'll have to think hard about which rules of behavior you no longer want to follow and how to handle the judgments that might come your way from others.

Now you might be thinking, "Keri and Kelly, don't judge me, but I don't think I'm self-concordant with all of my core values.

Some of them are more aspirational than actual at this point." We're not judging! It happens to everybody. Heck, we're all works in progress.

Then again, what are you waiting for? Even though perfection is never the goal (and we mean *never*), the more you work on making your values actual rather than aspirational, the more authentic you will be and the more you will become the person you want to be. The more you'll leave those nasty, old, unwanted expectations behind and fly out from the walls of your various boxes to a life of freedom.

For example, if one of your core values is Joy, recognizing that will help you make a more concerted effort to feel and express it more often. If one of your core values is Empathy, you might decide that you will work on being more empathetic and expressing it to others whenever the opportunity comes your way. You might reach out to a friend who's going through a hard time or notice when someone's feelings have been hurt and lend them an ear.

Our friend Bryce named Authenticity as one of his core values, but as he walked through his day-to-day life, he started to notice how often he was false. He was fine with telling a white lie if it spared someone's feelings, but he discovered that he pretended a lot more than he wanted. "I kept it from my wife that I didn't want to visit her parents one weekend when I was feeling particularly tired," he says. "I think I did this because I have always expected myself to keep my wife happy, but I think I try to do that at all costs. As a result, I have often felt resentful and later punished her by acting irritable and passive-aggressive. We have argued a lot because of this, and by expecting myself to keep her happy even if it means I'm not, I actually end up making us both unhappy." The next time Bryce wanted to skip a visit with his wife's parents, he lived by his core value of Authenticity and told her how he really felt. She was disappointed but understood. Bryce began to see how the expectation that he had to keep his wife happy all the time caused him to abandon his core value of Authenticity. By letting go of pretense, even in everyday situations, he released himself from a lot of stress. Yes, it was scary to be honest with people, especially his wife, but in most cases, it wasn't nearly as big a deal as he worried it would be.

Again, though, watch out for that nasty perfectionist on your shoulder. If one of your core values is Health, you might give yourself a break if you decide to enjoy a big slice of chocolate cake (and ice cream, of course). But it's different if you're deviating from your value several times a week, or if Charity is a core value, yet you never seem to make a charitable contribution. These are gaps that clearly need some attention.

## HONORING YOUR CORE VALUES AND BECOMING MORE *YOU*

Take another look at your top five core values and the boxes you created in chapter 1. How much is each of your values present in each area of your life right now?

- Family of Origin
- Religion/Spirituality
- Community/Culture
- Gender
- Love/Marriage
- Career/Work

For example, you might express/honor four of your core values with your family of origin but only two of them in your career/work.

Once you have named the values that are present in each area, ask yourself: *If a value isn't present in a particular area, do I want it to be?* You might not need every value to be a part of every aspect of your life.

If one of your core values is Challenge, but it isn't present in your career/work area, that might be one of the reasons why your Career box is smaller than you'd like. Let's say that at the end of the section on career (chapter 7), you discovered that you have expected yourself to be a diligent worker who stays quiet and doesn't make waves. After all, it's what your father did before you. But then you recall that he performed the same job for decades without advancement. Maybe the action you have to take to bring your value of Challenge into your career is to throw away the expectation that you don't make waves. Then, you can give yourself permission to speak to your supervisor about taking on more responsibility. Maybe you will even put your hat in the ring for a position that will allow you to grow and learn. It might not be easy to suddenly become outspoken, but in the next chapter, we'll walk you through an action plan in which you could prepare yourself for the conversation with your boss.

What if Pleasure is one of your core values, but you realize it's missing from all areas of your life? Think about how you can bring more pleasure into your life. Maybe painting, going to the theater, listening to live music, or spending time in nature give you pleasure. Can you schedule more of your favorite activities?

You might also find that circumstances sometimes cause you to shift a bit in how you go about living your core values (COVID-19, anyone?). That happened for our podcast guest Amy Evans, who told us that she shares the core value of Adventure with her partner. "It's really important to us that we're exploring and going on adventures," she said. "And when the pandemic started . . . we realized that the way that we define adventure, which is traveling and going far and wide to amazing exotic places, wasn't going to be available to us." So Amy shifted and found that creativity was a way she could satisfy her need for adventure. As a result, she tried painting for the first time. We thought this was ingenious.

If you're struggling to stay true to one of your core values in some aspect of your life, does Amy's creativity inspire an approach that you haven't thought about before? Brainstorm possibilities to see if you can come up with a way to honor your core values more.

## PRIORITIZE YOUR LIST OF UNWANTED EXPECTATIONS

At the end of the previous chapters, you determined which unwanted expectation was the most consequential for each category, whether family of origin, religion, love/marriage, and so on. But how do you decide which one to let go of first?

Well, as we've illustrated, getting to know your core values can help you make those kinds of decisions. We recommend, however, that you avoid starting with an expectation that's really going to upset the apple cart. Start with an easier one to get your feet wet. It will give you more confidence for working on the challenging ones.

But wait—how do you know which ones are easier and which ones will be difficult, as well as which ones will give you the most "bang for your buck"? To help you figure it out, we have adapted a traditional 2x2 priority grid for this purpose.

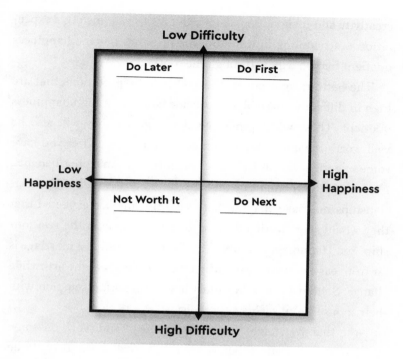

Go back to the one expectation that you pinpointed as the most consequential at the end of chapters 2, 3, 4, 5, 6, and 7. You will have a total of six unwanted expectations that you have chosen, and the 2x2 grid will help you decide which one you will let go of first.

The top right box of the grid is for expectations that are low stakes to address but will provide you with a high happiness quotient if they were gone. These are the expectations we recommend getting rid of first because they won't cause you a lot of stress but will quickly show you the benefits of releasing unwanted expectations. They are the easy wins! Here's an example: You listed Creativity/Imagination as one of your core values, but at the end of the career chapter, you noted your expectation that you maintain a stringent work ethic, which robs you of the time to express your creativity and imagination. All it will take to vanquish this expectation is scheduling in time to write or paint, but the happiness quotient for you will be through the roof!

The bottom right box of the grid is for expectations that are high in difficulty and will also provide you with a high happiness quotient. These will be more challenging, but they will also be well worth the effort. We recommend doing these after you have some experience with the easier ones that promise big benefits. An example here might be an expectation at the end of the relationships/marriage chapter. Let's say someone has expected that they would stay married despite feeling unhappy in the relationship. Yet, Happiness is a core value for them. Ending a marriage is far from easy, however, even when it's a necessary and worthwhile change. So they decide they must have a difficult discussion with their spouse about seeing a therapist.

Note that you might decide to go ahead and work on some "Do Later" expectations before your "Do Next" ones. It could be that a "Do Next" expectation is so difficult that it requires a lot of planning and psyching yourself up. If you decide you must end a relationship, for example, you will likely need more time before you make that kind of astronomical change in your life.

The top left box of the grid is for expectations that are low in difficulty but also low in happiness quotient. We recommend doing these last because while they might be easy, they won't provide as much satisfaction. Still, they might be worth doing. For example, you might have continued going to church because you felt it was expected in your community, but through reading this book, you realize you don't want to go anymore. It may not be a particularly consequential expectation, but you listed Authenticity as one of your core values. You want to be true to yourself. While someone might ask you why you're no longer at church, you don't really care if they judge you. Not going there anymore will hardly change your life, but it's still better than living according to an expectation that no longer makes sense based on who you are.

The bottom left box of the grid is for expectations that are high in difficulty but low in happiness quotient. We recommend that you not do these at all. If they're going to be very hard to release without providing much benefit, they aren't worth it. An example here might be an expectation that you must accept your mother's calls twice a day to check in with you. It's annoying, but only in a minor way. Still, discussing it with her would probably be quite painful because she'd feel very hurt. Compassion is on your list of core values, so for this one, you decide not to let go of the expectation at all. It just isn't worth the effort and consequences.

Here's what your grid might look like using our examples.

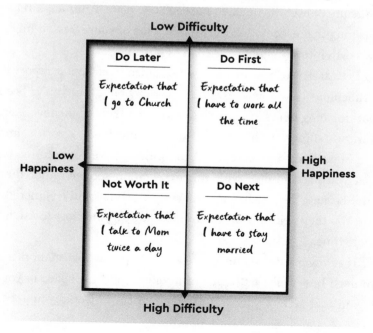

If you have a physical book, we give you permission to write in it. Otherwise, you can draw your own grid and write your expectations in it. Just note that if you're considering getting rid of an expectation that might prove difficult for someone else, don't write it down where it might be found before you have discussed your plans with them.

Since we have asked you to choose the expectation for each category that has been the most consequential for you, it's likely that all of them will end up on the right side of the grid with high happiness possibilities if you were to let them go. But you can use this grid for any other unwanted expectations. There will be others that fall into the low happiness categories, and this exercise can help you determine which ones can wait or aren't worth it at all.

It's also true that if a particular expectation is causing you a lot of stress, you may decide to prioritize it even if it's going to be high difficulty or even if you have a lot on your plate. After all, if relinquishing that expectation can relieve some of your stress, it might be worth it to say goodbye as soon as possible.

Let's say your boss expects you to finish a particular report in a ridiculous time frame. You can't possibly do it, but you've been working long hours and losing sleep as you try to somehow make it work. Telling your boss you need more time is also stressful, and you've wanted to avoid it at all costs. But you've come to realize that you need to deal with this expectation sooner rather than later because despite its high difficulty, the relief will feel incredible. You then prioritize the conversation with your boss to ask for more time.

If at any point you aren't sure where to put an expectation, ask yourself how much letting go of it will expand the space in your box in that area of your life. How much closer would you get to breaking down the walls and flying out of that particular box? You can also review your values list and ask yourself: *How much will giving up this expectation help me honor or express my core values?* This will tell you how much happiness you can gain from saying goodbye to that particular expectation.

## WHAT THE HELL DO YOU WANT MOST?

In some cases, it might be easy enough to just wave goodbye to an unwanted expectation and walk away, such as when you decide to tell someone you don't want to participate in a particular activity anymore and they express mild disappointment. But in other cases, you might feel like you're lost in the middle of a road that seems to lead to nowhere. What are you going to do if you think you might need a divorce, a split with your religion, or a new profession altogether? Phew! Those are mind-blowing.

When letting go of an expectation means a major change in your life, you have to at least begin to get a handle on what you want *instead*. Still, if you've spent your life living by certain expectations that you believed you had to maintain, freeing your mind to other possibilities can feel as foreign as traveling to Mars.

These kinds of changes will probably require some of that time "sitting your ass down quietly" to figure out what you want to do. Can you release an expectation and stay in your marriage, religion, or career? Or will you indeed have to leave, and what will that mean for you? These are big, challenging life decisions that no one should take lightly.

And if you've been in a stuffy box for a long time, you don't know what it's like to live free on the outside. It's a little like being released from jail, so it can be scary to step out of that box.

A friend of ours was happy in her profession for years . . . until she wasn't. When she finally gave herself permission to leave it, she was overwhelmed by the possibilities. What would she do instead? There were so many choices that it made her dizzy. It was exciting and terrifying at the same time.

Whenever you need to unearth what you truly want, besides your exploration of your core values (which will definitely help you), ask yourself these key questions:

1. What am I no longer willing to tolerate?

2. What am I most passionate about in my life?

3. What brings me the most joy, whether people, things, or activities? What delights me?

4. What makes me laugh?

5. How would I like to feel the most often?

6. If I think back to a time when my life was great, what values was I expressing or honoring the most? (For example, let's say one of your happiest memories is when you were a guest on your city's morning news show. The value you may pinpoint from that experience could be Daring because it took a lot of courage for you to do that interview.)

7. When have I felt the proudest?

8. When do I feel most like my true, authentic self? Who am I with, and what am I doing?

9. What helps me get up in the morning and feel ready to start my day?

10. How do I want to be remembered?

11. What am I most grateful for in my life?

Answering these questions can help you determine what you want instead of what you have now. They can help to move you past the limited thinking that has kept you stuck in your stuffy boxes. You have to take off the blinders and see possibilities where you didn't see them before. They are almost always there if you can just allow yourself to see them.

We'll end this chapter with thoughts from our podcast guest Eileen Tarjan. If you aren't happy with some aspect of your life, *have curiosity*. She says, "I'm always thinking I can't do something, but what if I could? I wonder what that would look like."

## SHHH . . . LISTEN TO THE QUIET VOICE

One of the ways that you can get in touch with what you really want is by learning how to hear the quiet voice inside yourself. Now, we aren't going to get all spiritual woo-woo with you, but we do sometimes get "woo adjacent." And this is one of those times.

In the last chapter, we told you about Andy Lee, who turned his mindfulness practice into a profession. He told us how much the practice helped him get in touch with his authenticity and what he really wanted. We recommend it, too. Not only is it a great way to slow down the usual chatter in your mind and hear what you truly want, but it can reduce stress, which has both mental and physical benefits.

If you have never tried mindfulness meditation, apps such as Headspace or Calm are a good way to start. And even if you have tried mindfulness in the past and it didn't work for you, give it another try. If you lean into it more, its power just might surprise you.

# CHAPTER 9
# Time to Take Action: Break Out of Your Boxes Like a Champion

Up to this point, we have focused on helping you gain awareness of the expectations that aren't working for you, what matters most to you (your values), and what you truly want. This awareness work is important because it helps you make good decisions when you let go of expectations you no longer want.

But if you gain awareness about your expectations and values without *ever* taking action, you'll just stay stuck in your little boxes, knowing that you could (dare we say *should*) break out, if you would only move forward. There's no denying that action is where you actually see results.

That's why this chapter is about the second to last letter of our BREAK process—ACTION—which is the actual *change* part of it all. It's about getting off your butt and making it happen.

Now some people are eager to let their superhero cape fly as they jump to the action part. But there are others of us (and you know who you are) who would just as soon sit down in our boxes and stay put for years. It can be scary outside of those walls.

If that sounds familiar, you will no doubt need to give yourself a little (or perhaps a hefty) push. Simply put, it's easy to *not* take action.

The two of us have worked with many people who have kick-ass ideas, but expectations (and resulting fears) often keep them trapped in their boxes where, let's face it, there isn't enough room to implement anything that's remotely kick-ass.

We hear this quote in sports consistently, "You miss 100 percent of the scores/goals/baskets you don't take." While we don't reference sports often, this quote is a wonderful reminder. At some point, you have to be like a good bird mama and push yourself out of the nest (or box, in this case) in order to take flight.

After all, if you're living by unwanted expectations, you aren't *really* comfortable, are you? You're just in a familiar place, and letting go of an expectation is unfamiliar (i.e., uncomfortable). But nine times out of ten, the discomfort of taking the action to say buh-bye to an expectation is short term, while the discomfort of staying in your box(es) for years (and maybe more years) is *long term*. Would you rather be temporarily uncomfortable or uncomfortable forever?

If you start to feel so overwhelmed that you find yourself plopping right back down into your particular box, *please, please* stop and take a breath. Don't put too many expectations on yourself about fucking the expectations! Be gentle with yourself as you figure out your next steps.

Think of your motivation like a rubber band. There has to be some tension for you to take action and move forward. But it doesn't work well if the band is stretched almost to the point of breaking. It also doesn't work if it's so slack that it just lays there doing nothing.

Our podcast guest Charlie Jones had a great idea that we absolutely love. The IT executive suggests choosing a theme song that spurs you to action and keeps you fired up. "Eye of the Tiger" by Survivor is the obvious choice that might come to mind for a certain generation. But others we thought of are "Firework" by Katy Perry, "Confident" by Demi Lovato, "We Are the Champions" by Queen, "Shake It Off" by Taylor Swift, or even "Let It Go" from *Frozen* if you don't have children who have made you too sick of it. Then there's the ultimate letting-go-of-expectations song, "How Far I'll Go" from the animated Disney film *Moana*.

But we don't want to forget those of us who might get so revved up that we run off half-cocked without an action plan. If you're prone to doing that, we ask you to also stop and take a breath. One of the important steps in this chapter is *planning*. The actions you take are much more likely to be successful if you think about them carefully beforehand and plot your path.

Even so, your first attempt might not work. It could just be a learning experience on the way to success. Sometimes, you solve one problem, only to create a new one that you have to address. This doesn't mean you've done it wrong; it's just life.

With all of that in mind, let's get started on your action plan to break out of those little boxes!

## SAYING A FINAL "GOODBYE" TO AN EXPECTATION

Let's say that after reading the previous chapters, you have come to realize that you don't want to accept the expectation from your friend to go out for a drink every Friday night after work. In this case, the action might simply be to say no. You just want to *not* do what they expect anymore. It might still be a bit scary, but it's taking an action when you say no and just stop an expectation in its tracks by not saying yes to it anymore.

But what if saying no in your situation is more complicated than that? This was the case for our friend Nigel. His sister had expected him to bail her out financially every time she overspent for nearly three years. "I feel like I was enabling her and preventing her from learning responsibility," he says. But he didn't have the heart to stop until he evaluated the expectations that he was living by and realized he needed to stop. "I was actually going into debt for the first time in my life because of my loans to my sister, so I've felt increasingly resentful about it," Nigel told us. "And it was out of alignment with my core value of Self-love."

A simple no in this situation probably wouldn't suffice, especially since he knew his mother would call to beg him to keep helping his sister out. "Of course, I do dread the conversations with my sister and mother," he admitted.

He knew if he didn't put some tension on his rubber band, he would just keep giving his sister money and letting his debt escalate. He was going to have to push himself out of the box by taking the actions necessary to drop this expectation.

He also knew that both his sister and his mom are master manipulators. They would try to convince him that he needed to continue this codependent practice. He wanted to be prepared and decided to address each of them separately. The first step of his action plan to crush this expectation was to write down what he would like to say. "I thought about what they might say in response and how their words might make me feel," he says. "I realized they would probably elicit my guilt and natural empathy. I wanted to be ready to handle these triggers, both emotionally and verbally. No matter what they would say, I decided to simply repeat my decision: 'I'm no longer willing or able to help out financially, and that's final.' And I refused to entertain questions about why."

The other thing Nigel knew about himself was that he tended to lose his temper whenever his mother and sister tried to manipulate him. The second step of his action plan was to call a trusted friend and ask them to role-play with him. They pretended to be his sister and then his mother as he told them what he had decided. This allowed him to practice keeping his cool. He knew he couldn't fully anticipate what they would say, but he could set himself up for success by being as emotionally and verbally ready for the discussions as possible. "My friend reminded me not to expect perfection from myself," he says. These would be high-stakes conversations, so all he could do was try to be the best version of himself that he could and then forgive himself if he fell short of his . . . yes, expectations.

The day of the call with his sister, he added more steps to his action plan: eating a nutritious, high-protein but light meal, talking with his friend to help him calm down, making himself a cup of chamomile tea, and meditating for a half hour with soothing music in the background. While neither conversation was pleasant, he stuck to his decision and got through it. "I started to lose my temper at one point with my sister," Nigel says, "but I took a breath and calmed myself down. It took awhile for them to forgive me, but eventually, they did. Sometimes, my sister tries to ask me for money again, but I simply reiterate my boundary. It hasn't been easy for me, but I'm no longer in debt or feeling stressed about the situation. It feels wonderful to stay in concordance with my core value of Self-love."

These kinds of boundary-making conversations with family or friends can be very difficult. If you struggle with boundaries, we can recommend two books that you might find helpful: *Setting Boundaries Will Set You Free: The Ultimate Guide to Telling the Truth, Creating Connection, and Finding Freedom* by Nancy Levin and *Set Boundaries, Find Peace: A Guide to Reclaiming Yourself* by Nedra Glover Tawwab.

Most actions that you want to take require more than one step, whether it's the process of saying goodbye to an expectation or implementing a new plan. As you saw with Nigel's situation, he went through several steps to rid himself of this expectation from preparing what he was going to say to practicing with his friend to meditating before the phone calls.

If you plan to change jobs or homes, for example, you will likely have a long list of steps that will be stretched out over time. It's important to write all your steps down (making adjustments whenever necessary).

We also recommend telling someone else you trust about your action plan. We'll talk more about accountability and gathering your tribe in the next chapter, but having people who support you in achieving your actions can make a big difference.

It helps immensely to break down your action plan into very small steps like Nigel did before he called his sister and mother. If you try to just work toward something big like "tell sister I won't help her financially anymore" or "find a new, enjoyable job," you might feel overwhelmed by the enormity of it and give up too quickly. You might feel lost as to what to do next. We tend to move forward faster when each step in our plan is bite-sized enough to be in reach.

As you complete each small step, evaluate your progress. Do

you seem to be on the path to alleviating your expectation and flying out of your box toward something new and wonderful, or do you need to course-correct and try something else?

## LET'S GET MOVING: CREATE *YOUR* ACTION PLAN

Review your work from chapter 8—your core values, your 2x2 grid of unwanted expectations, and your answers to the questions at the end of the chapter. Create an action plan for the first two expectations you have chosen.

Write down the expectation you want to eliminate, such as: *I have to live in the same city as my family.*

Start by asking yourself these questions and writing down your answers:

*What fears come up when I think about releasing this expectation and moving away?*

To help you manage your fears, can you remember a time in the past when you moved or succeeded in achieving something equally daunting?

What have you learned from past experiences that could help you be successful in making your move?

What would it feel like if you weren't afraid? Can you imagine it?

What is your theme song for making this move?

Once you have finished answering these questions, begin to plan how you will do it. Break down each step you need to take to reach it. Don't skip any steps but start with the easiest ones. That way, you'll be less likely to get overwhelmed. And you can always add more steps later if necessary. If thinking about the big move motivates you, think away. If it overwhelms you, keep your eye on the next step *only*.

Here's an example of what the beginning of your action plan might look like:

Expectation: *I have to live in the same city as my family.*
Ultimate Goal: *Move to a new city.*

## Action Plan:

1. Research cities that interest me. Who do I know in each place? What social and community possibilities do I have in each?

2. Research job possibilities in the cities that interest me.

3. Research real estate in the cities that interest me.

4. Make connections with people in companies where there might be a job for me and ask them what's available.

5. Narrow down my choices to the top two based on my research.

6. Visit my top two cities to check out real estate and get a feel for them.

7. Make a list of the pros and cons of living in each city.

8. Ask therapist or friend for help in deciding what to say to family about the move and practice the conversation with her.

9. Schedule the conversation with family.

10. Eat a healthy breakfast the morning before the conversation.

11. Exercise while listening to soothing music.

12. It's the big day! Take a deep breath and have the conversation with family.

13. Take a self-care day to recover from the emotional aftermath of the family conversation.

14. Begin to send résumés to potential employers in top two city choices.

15. If no results come from my first letters, send letters to my next choices.

16. Work with a friend or coach to help me prepare for interviews.

17. Set up interviews.

18. Field offers and decide on city where I will move. (Lucky Step!)

19. Look at houses or apartments.

20. Put in offers on chosen houses or apartments.

21. Create spreadsheet to keep up with offers.

The next steps might include choosing a place to live and moving date, packing up, and actually moving. This kind of change after releasing an expectation can be scary as hell, but also enormously exciting. That's how we felt when we moved to California. We were energized and so ready for it. At the same time, we constantly said, "OMG! OMG! OMG!" Kelly looked at seventy houses in Southern California and put offers on eleven of them. Trust us when we say that action step 21 was more than necessary. Spreadsheets, people!

Remember that you may make a misstep along the way and need to regroup. You may even have to learn new skills or get some help before you can complete all your steps. Tom Glaser, author of *Full Heart Living*, told us on our podcast that he tried a ropes course once that involved climbing up a telephone pole while you wear a safety harness. The first time he did it, he climbed up the rungs and tried to stand on the top of the pole, but he fell immediately. "I went too fast," he thought. Before he tried it a second time, he asked the guy helping him with the harness to give him advice.

The man gave him some hints, and Tom was able to stand on top of the pole the next time without falling. Never hesitate to ask for help. Don't *expect* yourself to do it alone!

## LET'S TALK ABOUT TIME

When you set a goal and engage in an action plan, it's customary to give yourself a specific timeline. We've definitely noticed that when we set a date to finish something, we're much more likely to finish it. A sense of urgency toward reaching a specific deadline helps to keep you motivated and working on the steps of your plan.

That said, time can either be your friend or your enemy. It's your friend if it keeps your eye on the prize without making you crazy. It's your enemy if you set a deadline that you can't meet without rushing decisions and possibly making mistakes along the way. Allow your deadline to be fluid and changeable if it needs to be. Give yourself that grace if you can't honor the first timeline you set.

On the other hand, resist the temptation to allow yourself to push your deadline later and later because you're afraid of finishing your action plan. If you find yourself putting off your deadline for too long, remember your "why"—the reason you're eliminating this expectation and following this action plan toward something better for you. Work on diminishing your fears as much as you can and get help if you need it. Sometimes, talking it out with someone else is just what you need to feel fired up and moving toward your goal again.

## Some Final Tips to Help You Along

Before we leave you to create your own action plan, we have a few more tips. First, visualize yourself crushing the expectation, making terrific choices, and handling your success well. If nothing else, this practice helps to dissipate fears and increase your motivation. Give it a try!

If you struggle with a choice between two or more possibilities, revisit the questions in the "What the Hell Do You Want Most?" section of chapter 8.

And if you ever start to hunker back down in your box and think about keeping an expectation you *know* you need to let go, visualize what your life will be like if you maintain that status quo. Will you have the wedding your mother wants and regret not having the one *you* wanted . . . for the rest of your life? Will you retire from the job you hate and never find out what your life would've been like if you followed your dream?

Our final piece of advice about your action plan is to celebrate every little win along the way. Don't just plan a big celebration when you reach the finish line. Treat yourself when you complete every few steps. It's one of the best ways we know to stay motivated and on track!

Now it's your turn. What steps will you need to take to vanquish your expectation?

When you're ready, turn the page, and let's talk about the last letter of the **BREAK** process so that you *keep* it going and avoid falling back into the habit of abiding by unwanted expectations.

# CHAPTER 10

# Keep It Going and Live Free!

Actress Viola Davis has said, "It is your job in life to disappoint as many people as you can so you do not disappoint yourself." Fucking the expectations is often about that very thing. It's important to remember this because it's so easy to fall back into the soft arms of the unhealthy homeostasis you're used to. But if the old expectations have left you disappointed and unhappy, it doesn't make sense to allow yourself to go back to them just because they're comfortable and familiar. Or just because they prevent someone *else* from feeling disappointed. We are all about giving to others, but there's a way to be generous without letting yourself down.

One of Kelly's coaching clients recently talked about "protecting your peace." Not disappointing yourself protects your peace, and that's one of the ways you ensure that you make the most of this life. Too often, we're so frightened of causing conflict and losing our *short-term* peace that we sacrifice our *long-term* peace, sometimes for years.

This final chapter is about keeping up the changes you have made and staying out of your tiny boxes so that you don't lose ground. It's the final letter in the BREAK process and the post-change phase that people also tend to skip. It's about living your life free of expectations and doing whatever the hell you want on a regular basis. After all, it isn't enough to have an escape plan if you walk right back into jail, and unfortunately, a lot of people do just that if they don't pay attention to this last piece of the process.

When you let go of expectations, you also let go of the status quo and perhaps the unhealthy homeostasis that you may have been a part of within your family, religion, or culture. The new state of being might feel uncomfortable at first—sort of like new shoes you have to break in. Give yourself time to become accustomed to this new you. People may continue to push back, trying to get you to abide by their expectations again. And hey, even if everything goes very well, it can be uncomfortable at first just because it's unfamiliar. It can take time to get used to success. It takes fortitude to keep it going and stay out of those boxes!

You might also feel regret if, for example, you believe you spent years in a job because of a bullshit expectation. You might feel like you wasted a lot of time. But please don't go there. We can't do better until we know better, and we're all in the school of life, learning as we go. You made a different choice once you had the data, and you simply didn't have that data before. Avoid ruminating on the past or comparing yourself to anyone else—it is a surefire path to unhappiness.

Depending on the expectations you vanquish, you might also experience some grief and loss. You may have to give up something or someone in order to be true to yourself. Give yourself grace and time to recover from that. There's nothing easy about it.

Now that you're more attuned to expectations all around you, we suspect you'll notice them more and more—in the complaints your friends share with you, in conversations you hear between other people, and in the news. Expectations are often fodder for both comedy and drama in novels, television shows, and movies. The popular television comedy *The Marvelous Mrs. Maisel,* for example, was largely about gender and family expectations.

Keep your theme song handy as your rallying cry whenever you need motivation to stick to your escape plan and make sure those expectations stay duly fucked. If you like, find yourself a new theme song that speaks to your upgraded state of being. (There are lots of songs with "freedom" in the title.)

Let's talk about some of our other main tips for staying free of expectations.

## THE REST RESISTANCE

We have reminded you about the importance of not *expecting* perfection of yourself (or anybody else for that matter). Just as you should avoid pushing yourself to exhaustion while working on your action plans, remember not to push too hard while reinforcing the changes you have implemented. Each of us has to learn what we need to rest, recharge, and refuel. And those needs will change as you age and go through difficult challenges. If you've just experienced a loss, you'll need more time and care before you can function again like the champion you are.

In American culture, we seem to have developed such a resistance to rest that the phrase *rest resistance* was coined in the popular book *Rest Is Resistance: A Manifesto* by Tricia Hersey, founder of the Nap Ministry. On the Nap Ministry's website, it says, "*Rest Is Resistance* is a call to action and manifesto for those who are sleep deprived, searching for justice, and longing to be liberated from the oppressive grip of Grind Culture."[1] Can you relate? Grind Culture seems to be a particularly American phenomenon.

In some parts of the world, for example, people take a three-hour lunch to recharge in the middle of the day. For most of us in the US, this practice feels like blasphemy! Instead, we work, work, and work some more. We push, push, and then wonder why we get sick. And if we do slow down, we feel guilty about it, thinking we didn't do enough. We might even accuse ourselves of being lazy. But according to Devon Price, PhD, the author of *Laziness Does Not Exist*, we do more work today than our ancestors ever did at any other time in history. Why do we still feel like we aren't doing enough?

While you're progressing and making sure you don't fall back into old expectation habits, don't push yourself into oblivion. In other words, remember that you aren't a machine! Even a Porsche has to refuel (or recharge if it's electric). And have you ever heard a Porsche say, "I'm sorry I'm lazy; I need to refuel"? Nope, a Porsche has never felt lazy or guilty. *In this respect, be like a Porsche.*

## HABITS AND HEALTH

Back in the 1600s, the poet John Dryden said, "We first make our habits, and then our habits make us." He wasn't wrong. Duke University researchers say that 40 percent of our behaviors are habits.[2] That's a lot of time spent doing the same things and possibly making ourselves healthy or unhealthy, happy or unhappy, depending on the habits we are perpetuating. Making sure your habits are good ones will help you reinforce what you have accomplished.

Habit expert James Clear says willpower is like a muscle, so it will get tired and sore if you try to start with lifting the highest weight. Instead, if you want to change a bad habit into a better one, you have to start with what's easy and build up to it. It's similar to what we suggested for your steps on your action plan. You're much more likely to succeed if the new habit isn't something you have to take on all at once. This means breaking down habits into small pieces just like you broke down your plans. Then, allow yourself to improve in tiny increments and acknowledge each small improvement.

When you slip up, don't let it derail you. Shake it off and start again with your new habit. It even helps to plan for potential slips. What might throw you off course, and what can you do to prevent it? If you do slip, what can you do to help yourself bounce back? Then, be patient with yourself. The latest research says it can take months to solidify a new habit.[3]

For example, if you're a woman, maybe you want to break free of the expectation that you need to be a superhero and do it all. You have to be the high-powered career woman, the perfect wife, the best mom, and a sexual dynamo in the bedroom. Maybe you start with breaking a small habit, like choosing not to stay up late to clean the house. Maybe you just clean for fifteen minutes a day. Then, you build on that over time, changing more tiny habits until you kick that Wonder Woman expectation to the curb.

Of course, there's no getting around the fact that reinforcing the changes you want will be easier if you're as healthy as possible. So besides avoiding rest resistance, pay attention to your body and what it needs. If your body is exhausted, you'll find it much harder to clean the house at all or to kick ass at the office. If your body feels good, you'll not only be able to kick ass when you want but enjoy your life more, too.

## ARE YOUR FRIENDS HELPING YOU STAY FREE?

Sometimes, when we give expectations the middle finger, our friends are unwilling to come along for the ride. Again, while you don't want to disappoint a friend, isn't it worse to disappoint yourself when it means going against who you are or something you want very much? Plus, it's much harder to keep up your momentum when friends try to pull you back or keep you down.

When Kelly moved to California, it wasn't just her parents who were unhappy with the idea. Her good friend Diane was also less than thrilled. She said to Kelly, "I don't know why you would make a change like this. Your entire family's here. You'll never come out and see us again."

Kelly thought Diane would surely come to her senses within a day or two and realize she had lashed out because she didn't want to lose her friend. But Diane didn't take back what she said, and their relationship fell apart. It was sad, but Kelly told her, "I'm not going to stay in Wisconsin because you're unhappy about my move. I have to do what I need to make myself happy."

Sometimes, the longer you've sustained a friendship, the harder it is to break free. You've invested a lot of time in this person, so it might feel like failure if you give up. But the truth is that the longer a friendship goes on, the greater the possibility you will outgrow it.

We're not trying to be callous and imply that friendships are transactional or disposable. Nevertheless, it's important to ask if a relationship is bringing you down or providing you with a beautiful energy (like the friendship the two of us have, which we're happy to openly brag about). Of course, none of your friends will be perfect 24/7, never getting on your nerves or pissing you off. Nobody could pass that hard a test, and all relationships require compromise. But if the scales regularly tip toward the negative more than the positive, it might be time to seriously rethink the friendship.

If you're struggling with a particular friend, ask yourself: Does this person help me be a better version of myself and vice versa? Do they support me in letting go of unwanted expectations? Do we share values? Do we share our feelings and beliefs respectfully and disagree in a healthy way? Can we be authentic with each other? Do we trust each other? Do we have a good time together? Do we each devote relatively equal time and effort to the relationship?

When you see your friend's name pop up on your phone, what does your body tell you? Do you feel tense or happy? In a survey, 84 percent of women and 75 percent of men said that they'd had a toxic friend at least once in their lives.[4] That's most of us!

Unhealthy friendships can have a detrimental effect on our mental and physical health, but good friendships feed us in ways that nothing else can. Supportive friends have even been found to help us reduce mortality rates by as much as 50 percent,[5] and being social can reduce our likelihood of getting common illnesses like a cold.[6] In short, good friends help you live longer, so maybe send your bestie some flowers.

We highly recommend surrounding yourself with wonderful friends, mentors, and colleagues. We like to call them your personal "board of directors." For some of us, they are our *chosen* family, especially if we have had to break ties with actual family members.

They are invaluable people to have in your corner, whether they help you with personal or professional matters.

On our podcast, Alli Trussell, an executive at a fast-growing SaaS company, said, "I'm a collector of really good, really smart humans, and I keep them close. And they are experts in their field. I'm not professionally trained in what I do. I'm very self-taught, and a lot of that has been through phenomenal mentors—people I have met along the way, people I've been lucky enough to work side by side with, and people who have taught me a lot of the skills that I use in my day-to-day job." And we can watch for allies everywhere we go.

Dr. Denise Moore Revel told us on the podcast about how she met an unexpected ally who gave her the impetus she needed to start her Own Your Amazing coaching practice. She was attending a women's conference where each attendee, one by one, went on stage for coaching about both their careers and their personal lives. Each one cried as they sat in the hot seat. Denise was sure she wouldn't cry, but suddenly, in that seat, she found herself bursting into tears. "I'm just not happy," she told the coach.

The night before the conference, Denise had shared dinner with a fellow attendee she had just met. While she was crying, her dinner companion raised her hand in the audience and said, "I know what's wrong with you!"

Denise immediately thought, "After one dinner, how could you possibly know me well enough to say that?"

But the woman said, "You're smart, you're brilliant, you're talented. You're all these things, but you don't own it. You need to own your amazing and stop playing small."

This stranger became an ally in that moment when she said out loud what Denise had not yet had the courage to tell herself, let alone anyone else. She was ready to transition from her work as a speech-language pathologist and become a life coach. Within two weeks of that experience, she planned and gave her first Own Your Amazing workshop to help women awaken their true potential. One of the things the experience in the conference taught Denise is that we sometimes expect too little of ourselves. We expect less than what we're capable of doing and giving. It's our friends, mentors, and sometimes even strangers who become new friends/allies who often help us see what's truly amazing about us.

That's one of the things the two of us do for each other. We both feel we're better people because the other one is in our lives. We like to think that ours is a wonderful friendship, and we hope you have this kind of friendship in your life, too. If you don't, please seek it out.

For example, we can call each other no matter what, whether we want to say, "Oh shit, I had a rough day and need to talk through it" or "I had the greatest thing happen and I want to share it with you."

We aren't perfect, but we work at our friendship. We give to each other because we want to, not because we feel obligated. And you'd better believe we make each other laugh . . . all the time! But we're just as comfortable when one, or both, of us needs to cry.

We also keep each other accountable when we're working on relinquishing an expectation and implementing an action plan. As you're working on yours, an "accountability buddy" will be *every-thing*. Tell someone you trust about your plan—someone who will cheer you on, not discourage you. A good friend or mentor will usually do even more than just cheer you on—they will give you gentle pushes to keep going and not give up. They will help you reinforce the changes you've made and live free of the expectations you have previously fucked. Like a great gymnastics coach, they will help you stick the landing.

## BECOMING YOU 2.0

Whenever we feel ourselves going off course, we reconnect with our values and authenticity—the person we truly are without undue expectations on our back. Then, we focus on the person we would like to become. Brad Carlson told us a story on our podcast that really stuck with us. He was in the middle of a divorce, and sitting on his couch one day he tried to call his cocker spaniel over to him. The dog wouldn't budge. "He just looked at me like I'm a total loser," Brad says. "Then, I realized I have to focus on what I want to become and who I want to be. And that decision changed my life forever."

Because of that moment, Brad came to terms with the fact that his attitude had destroyed his marriage. It all became crystal clear to him. He had been focusing on what he *didn't* want to be rather than what he *did* want to be. He no longer wanted to be a grumpy, lethargic couch potato. Instead, he wanted to focus on becoming upbeat, optimistic, outgoing, and energetic. He became hyper-determined and worked hard to transform his mindset.

What Brad also learned and now teaches is that we can make tangible changes in our lives, like eating a healthier diet or changing jobs, but a lot of what needs to change is *intangible*—how we think about ourselves and life. We must work to develop qualities like "determination, perseverance, commitment, focus, and courage."

Due to that pivotal moment in his life, Brad went on to train in the Unbeatable Mind mental toughness program with US Navy

Seal (Ret.) Mark Divine and worked with Tony Robbins. Eventually, he published his first book, *MindStrong*, and began to lead his MindStrongFit "P.O.W.E.R." mindset training seminars.

Brad says the biggest decision you will ever make in your life is choosing who you want to be and making a commitment to become that person.

Who do you want to be? What expectations need to go, and what do you need to do to stay that person for the rest of your life?

## WE'RE RAISING A GLASS TO YOUR FREEDOM!

No more suffocating boxes. No more dissatisfaction. No more status quo expectations. No more living someone else's life. No more abiding by someone else's rules. No more disappointing yourself in order to avoid disappointing others. *No more.*

This life belongs to no one but you. It's your time to live it as you choose. If someone else is unhappy with that, it's their problem. (Excuse us, but why aren't they focusing on their own life?)

We hope these pages have given you some awareness, some tools, some inspiration, and some laughs to help you begin to leave behind unwanted expectations and grab what you truly want.

We've said a lot about expecting too much of yourself. But we also hope you aren't expecting too little of yourself like Dr. Denise did, especially if others have told you that you *can't* or *shouldn't*. With that in mind, we'd like to leave you with one more story from our podcast.

Raymond D. Kemp Sr. has to be one of the most inspiring interviews we've ever had. As Fleet Master Chief for the US Navy, he met almost every American president who has been in office during his adulthood. He represented the Navy at the NATO

International Command Senior Enlisted Leader Conference, which included briefing over two hundred military leaders from African and European nations on leadership development and the value of cooperative agreements. As an Inspector General, he mentored more than three hundred junior executives monthly on leadership, best practices, and ethics at the Naval Leadership and Ethics Command and Senior Enlisted Academy. He spearheaded the repeal of Don't Ask, Don't Tell through face-to-face discussions with every crew member under his command for the purpose of building trust and resilience. Throughout his career, he has completed combat deployments that included participating in Operation Desert Storm. He has earned numerous awards, ribbons, and warfare medals. Now retired after thirty-three years in the Navy, he serves as a leadership coach for CEOs and professional athletes.

But if Raymond had paid attention to the low expectations that so many people had of him throughout his life, he never would have achieved so much. He was raised by a single mom, and his biological father wasn't in his life. Early on, a teacher said to him, "You're not going to be anything when you grow up. You're going to be like your dad, and you don't even know who that is." This teacher wanted him to think he wouldn't be able to do better than his father, who left the family, and that he wasn't worth anything just because he had never met his dad.

He could have allowed that statement to throw him smack-dab into a tiny, smothering box where he expected no more of himself than this teacher. (A lousy teacher, we might add.) But his mother was what he calls a "fierce angel." She and his grandmother encouraged him to believe that if he had the right attitude and tried his best, he could attain whatever he wanted.

His family didn't have the money to send him to college, so at age seventeen, he decided to join the Navy. He wasn't prepared for what would happen after boot camp when he met with an officer who would give him an assignment on his ship. Certainly, as a Black kid growing up in the 1960s and 1970s, Raymond was accustomed to hearing the notorious "n" word. But it was shocking to hear it in 1986 from his superior. When he entered the office, he saw a Texas Longhorns flag and a Confederate flag on display. He was supposed to be working as a data processing technician, but the officer behind the desk said, "I don't allow no n****** in my computer room." Instead, Raymond was sent to an area where he had to do manual labor.

There are situations when it makes sense to speak up about expectations and situations when you need to just bide your time. Raymond has said, "In my life, it has been very important for me to have my hand on the thermostat of my attitude." After all, our attitude is the one thing we can control. When this happened to him, he held on tightly to that thermostat.

"The thing is, I joined the Navy with the intention of doing twenty years and then going back to Oklahoma," he says. "The decision to press on toward my goal in spite of what he [the officer] said changed the trajectory of my life."

Raymond noted that Black soldiers were often getting passed over for advancement in the Navy. Still, he was determined not to be stopped by the low expectations that others placed on him merely because of his race. And he did rise through the ranks in spite of the odds until at the time of his retirement, he was the most senior Black person in the entire US Navy.

When he reached the rank to be a part of the board that selected people for various positions, he saw that there was still a great deal of discrimination—not just racial discrimination, but prejudice toward women and known LGBTQIA+ people as well. While there, he did what he could to make a dent in getting rid of these practices. "I was taught long ago that there will be occasions where you plant trees that bear fruit that you'll never taste," Raymond says.

"I challenge the status quo, and I challenge traditional thinking," he says. He seems to feel this is part of his job as a human being. His philosophy is that as long as we persevere, we can still get to whatever the goal may be. Raymond has certainly proven that in his own life, and his example is a great inspiration to us.

—

You've read on these pages about the diverse people we've met on our podcast and elsewhere who have fucked the expectations and broken out of their boxes to freedom. And we can personally attest to the power of living your life on your own terms and nobody else's.

As Raymond's story shows, it doesn't matter where you came from or where you started. You can create a better life for yourself if you refuse to live based on limiting expectations. And that's whether those expectations are coming from your parents, your boss, your partner, your religion, your community, or even your own head. If expectations have ruled your life, that can end now. Make "No, you can't" and "Stop, you shouldn't" phrases of the past. They're no longer a part of your vocabulary.

It's time to break down the walls of your little boxes and fly right out of there. You do deserve happiness, security, joy, peace, and to live authentically as nobody but YOU. This is your permission slip to do whatever the hell you want! Your life is yours.

# Acknowledgments

Gratitude overflows as we extend our heartfelt appreciation to the incredible individuals who have played pivotal roles in making this book a success. Foremost among them is Melanie Votaw, whose unwavering dedication, countless hours of listening, laughter, and meticulous writing and rewriting have not only contributed to the fruition of our passion project but have also brought our vision to life. Melanie, your talent is truly remarkable, and witnessing it firsthand has been a privilege beyond words.

Our journey began with a call to Maggie Langrick at Wonderwell, a pivotal moment that sparked the idea of translating our podcast into a book. The ensuing book retreat, orchestrated by the amazing team at Wonderwell—Maggie, Eva Avery, Jennifer Jensen, J Cisneros—became a transformative experience, fostering invaluable friendships and garnering unwavering support. Your mantra, "trust the creative process," became our guiding light, propelling us forward. And to our retreat besties, Bev Attfield and Pam Kling (PK), we experienced every emotion during our book retreat, and you were both there for us. We've learned so much from both of you. Thank you for truly embodying what it means to live your life on your terms.

A heartfelt acknowledgment is also due to our podcast guests, the unsung heroes of this journey. Your willingness to share vulnerable stories has not only enriched our podcasts but has been the wellspring of inspiration for this book. To each guest, you are unequivocally bad-asses, and we celebrate you!

Our deepest thanks to everyone who has been part of this incredible journey.

## KELLY'S PERSONAL ACKNOWLEDGMENTS

To my family for their unconditional love and support. To my mom and dad for trusting me when I've made decisions that you may not have always agreed with—but you always stood behind and supported me. Thank you for raising me to know how very blessed I am and that with hard work and dedication, good things can (and do) happen.

To Julie and Andrew, thank you for being the anchors that remind me to slow down and savor the beauty of each moment. Summers at Berry Lake—a treasure trove of shared memories and the warmth of genuine connection. Whether it's being a comforting presence or sharing in laughter, you uplift my spirit. To both of you, I express my deepest love and appreciation.

To Keri for being my best friend, business partner, podcast co-host, and now, co-author! Thank you for taking a chance on me all those years ago and look where it took us! I can't imagine being on this ride with anyone else. Your unwavering support, boundless creativity, and genuine friendship have been the pillars of our shared success. You're not just a business partner, you're a confidante who has stood with me through every triumph and challenge. You inspire me to be a better person every day. Thank you for being the extraordinary person you are, and I look forward to what the future holds—and of course, your multitude of ideas!

To my Grandma Nold for continuing to serve as an inspiration to me. Though we enjoyed a short time together, you left an indelible mark on my life and for that I'm eternally grateful.

## KERI'S PERSONAL ACKNOWLEDGMENTS

Here's to you, Kelly—my bestie, personal coach, cheerleader, and the one who makes every entrepreneurial challenge an exciting adventure. Through our partnership, we've not only dared to dream but turned those dreams into reality—launching a business, creating a podcast, and now, birthing a (I know it will be) successful book. Thanks for choosing this path with me, for believing in our dreams, and for hustling side by side. Our success is a testament to the power of our partnership.

My son, Roman, is an absolute source of inspiration in my life. His profound self-awareness and unwavering commitment to what brings him and does not bring him joy stands as a testament to his authenticity. Roman doesn't conform to anyone else's expectations. I cannot wait to watch him grow and defy societal norms, embracing his unique path with courage and determination. Roman, continue to be true to yourself—you are a beacon of authenticity. My love for you transcends words, and I am privileged to be your mother.

And to my husband, Steve, you are the most extraordinary person to have ever graced my life's path. During times when I was plagued with self-doubt, you believed in me, recognizing the creativity, passion, and love that resided within. Your creative soul, unwavering integrity, and steadfast loyalty serve as constant inspirations in my life. Moreover, your humor and adventurous spirit ensure we are never bored! I love you, Steve.

# Bibliography

1. Amato, Lori. "What Is the Average Number of Career Changes in a Person's Lifetime?" *Unmudl*, April 4, 2023, https://unmudl.com/blog/average-career-changes.

2. Anderson, Scott. "The Correlation Between Change Management and Project Success." *Prosci* (blog). Updated October 2, 2023, www.prosci.com/blog/the-correlation-between-change-management-and-project-success.

3. Bass-Kreuger, Maude. "Everything You Ever Wanted to Know About the White Wedding Dress." *Vogue*, July 22, 2020, www.vogue.co.uk/gallery/history-of-the-white-wedding-dress.

4. Beshesti, Naz. "Toxic Influence: An Average of 80% of Americans Have Experienced Emotional Abuse." *Forbes*, May 15, 2020, www.forbes.com/sites/nazbeheshti/2020/05/15/an-average-of-80-of-americans-have-experienced-emotional-abuse/?sh=3da74d697b49.

5. Bowley, Rachel. "Women's Equality Day: A Look at Women in the Workplace in 2017." *LinkedIn Official Blogs* (blog), August 28, 2017, https://blog.linkedin.com/2017/august/28/womens-equality-day-a-look-at-women-in-the-workplace-in-2017.

6. Centers for Disease Control and Prevention, "Suicide Data and Statistics." *CDC.gov*. April 6, 2023, www.cdc.gov/suicide/suicide-data-statistics.html.

7. Clear, James. "How to Build a New Habit: This Is Your Strategy Guide." *JamesClear.com*. https://jamesclear.com/habit-guide.

8. Cohen, Sheldon, William J. Doyle, et al. "Sociability and Susceptibility to the Common Cold." *Psychological Science* 14(5) (2003): 389–395, https://doi.org/10.1111/1467-9280.01452.

9. DePaolo, Bella, PhD. "Why So Many Women Are Perfectly Happy to Stay Single." *Psychology Today* (blog), October 29, 2018, www.psychologytoday.com/us/blog/living-single/201810/why-so-many-women-are-perfectly-happy-to-stay-single.

10. Gettysburg College. "One Third of Your Life Is Spent at Work." Gettysburg College website, www.gettysburg.edu/news/stories?id=79db7b34-630c-4f49-ad32-4ab9ea48e72b.

11. Holt-Lunstad, Julianne, Timothy B. Smith, and J. Bradley Layton. "Social Relationships and Mortality Risk: A Meta-Analytic Review." *PLoS Medicine* (2010), 7(7), e1000316. doi:10.1371/journal.pmed.1000316.

12. Janin, Alex. "The New Science on Making Healthy Habits Stick." *The Wall Street Journal*, September 27, 2023, www.wsj.com/health/wellness/healthy-habits-research-science-7f373f67.

13. Janiuha-Jivraj, Dr. Shaheena. "The Daddy Dilemma, Why Fatherhood Is Still a Penalty for Men's Careers." *Forbes*, May 16, 2023, www.forbes.com/sites/shaheenajanjuhajivrajeurope/2023/05/16/the-daddy-dilemma-why-fatherhood-is-still-a-penalty-for-mens-careers/?sh=33c074b841bc.

14. Jones, Jeffrey M. "U.S. Church Membership Falls Below Majority for First Time." *Gallup*, March 29, 2021, https://news.gallup.com/poll/341963/church-membership-falls-below-majority-first-time.aspx.

15. Kauflin, Jeff. "Only 15% of People Are Self-Aware—Here's How to Change." *Forbes*, May 10, 2017, https://www.forbes.com/sites/jeffkauflin/2017/05/10/only-15-of-people-are-self-aware-heres-how-to-change/?sh=3a917c952b8c.

16. Kininmonth, Christine. "Adam Alter's 'Anatomy of a Breakthrough' Summary." *The Growth Faculty*, June 21, 2023, www.thegrowthfaculty.com/blog/adamalteranatomyofbreakthrough.

17. Kirchgaessner, Stephanie. "Pope Francis: Not Having Children Is Selfish." *The Guardian*, February 11, 2015, www.theguardian.com/world/2015/feb/11/pope-francis-the-choice-to-not-have-children-is-selfish.

18. Lagarde, Christine, and Jonathan D. Ostry. "When More Women Join the Workforce, Everyone Benefits. Here's Why." *World Economic Forum*, December 4, 2018, www.weforum.org/agenda/2018/12/economic-gains-from-gender-inclusion-even-greater-than-you-thought.

19. Leonhardt, Megan. "American Women Are Increasingly the Breadwinner. But Many Are Still in Charge of Childcare, Cooking, and Cleaning." *Fortune*, April 13, 2023, https://fortune.com/2023/04/13/more-american-women-becoming-breadwinners.

20. Lockman, Dr. Darcy. "What 'Good' Dads Get Away With." *The New York Times*, May 4, 2019, www.nytimes.com/2019/05/04/opinion/sunday/men-parenting.html.

21. Loeb, Emily L., Jessica Kansky, et al. "Perceived Psychological Control in Early Adolescence Predicts Lower Levels of Adaptation into Mid-Adulthood." *Child Development*. (2021), 92(2), e158–e172, doi:10.1111/cdev.13377.

22. Malinsky, Gili. "'Work Is the Most Important Way of Proving Your Worth,' and It's Making Americans Miserable: Professor." *CNBC*, January 26, 2022, www.cnbc.com/2022/01/26/work-is-the-most-important-way-of-proving-your-worth-in-the-us-says-professor.html.

23. Nap Ministry. "Rest Is Resistance: A Manifesto." *The Nap Ministry*. https://thenapministry.com.

24. Neal, David, Wendy Wood, and Jeffrey Quinn. "Habits—A Repeat Performance. Performance." *Current Directions in Psychological Science* (2006), 15(4), https://doi.org/10.1111/j.1467-8721.2006.00435.x.

25. Orth, Taylor. "Does Society Pressure Men and Women to Have Children?" *YouGov*, (February 8, 2022, https://today. yougov.com/topics/politics/articles-reports/2022/02/08/ does-society-pressure-men-and-women-have-children.

26. Pew Research Center, "Religious Landscape Study." *Pew Research Center*. (2014), www.pewresearch.org/religion/ religious-landscape-study/views-about-homosexuality.

27. Pillemer, Karl, PhD. *Fault Lines: Fractured Families and How to Mend Them*. New York: Avery, 2022.

28. Pocock, Joanna. "Not So Lonely: Busting the Myth of the Only Child." *JSTOR Daily*, November 8, 2015, https://daily.jstor.org/ myth-lonely-only-child.

29. Potts, Monica. "Are Americans Unhappy?" *FiveThirtyEight*, March 28, 2022, https://fivethirtyeight.com/features/ are-americans-unhappy/.

30. PRB. "Research Shows Moms with Husbands or Live-In Male Partners Do More Housework Than Single Moms." *PRB*, May 8, 2019, www.prb.org/news/mothers-day.

31. Prince Harry, the Duke of Sussex. *Spare*. New York: Random House, 2023.

32. Renner, Ben. "Fathers Today More Engaged with Their Kids 'Than Ever Before,' Study Finds." *StudyFinds*, June 19, 2022, https://studyfinds.org/ fathers-more-engaged-with-kids-than-ever-before.

33. Reuters. "Husbands Create 7 Hours of Extra Housework for Their Wives." *HuffPost*, February 19, 2016, www.huffpost.com/ entry/husbands-create-7-hours-of-extra-housework-for-their- wives_n_56c72146e4b0ec6725e23e2c.

34. Rich, John D., Jr., PhD. "Strict Gender Roles Hurt Men, Too." *Psychology Today* (blog), March 21, 2018, www. psychologytoday.com/us/blog/parenting-purpose/201803/ strict-gender-roles-hurt-men-too.

35. Ringwald, Molly. "What About 'The Breakfast Club'?" *The New Yorker*, April 6, 2018, www.newyorker.com/culture/personal-history/what-about-the-breakfast-club-molly-ringwald-metoo-john-hughes-pretty-in-pink.

36. Sheldon, Kenneth M., Richard M. Ryan, et al. "Trait Self and True Self: Cross-Role Variation in the Big-Five Personality Traits and Its Relations with Psychological Authenticity and Subjective Well-Being." *Journal of Personality and Social Psychology* (1997), 73(6), 1380–1393, https://doi.org/10.1037/0022-3514.73.6.1380.

37. Statista Research Department. "Percentage of Childless Women in the United States in 2020, By Age." *Statista*, June 2, 2023, www.statista.com/statistics/241535/percentage-of-childless-women-in-the-us-by-age/#:~:text=In%202020%2C%2097.2%20percent%20of,44%20years%20old%20were%20childless.

38. Tajfel, Henri, M.G. Billig, et al. "Social Categorization and Intergroup Behaviour." *European Journal of Social Psychology* (1971), 1(2), 149–178, https://doi.org/10.1002/ejsp.2420010202.

39. Trompenaars, Fons, and Charles Hampden-Turner. *Riding the Waves of Culture: Understanding Diversity in Global Business*. Boston: Nicholas Brealey Publishing, 2020.

40. U.S. Surgeon General. "Our Epidemic of Loneliness and Isolation." (2023), www.hhs.gov/sites/default/files/surgeon-general-social-connection-advisory.pdf, 24.

41. Vanderkam, Laura. "Why Offering Paid Maternity Leave Is Good for Business." *Fast Company*, September 27, 2016, www.fastcompany.com/3064070/why-offering-paid-maternity-leave-is-good-for-business.

42. Wadley, Jared. "Men, Women Ride the Same Emotional Roller Coaster." *University of Michigan News*, October 25, 2021, https://news.umich.edu/men-women-ride-the-same-emotional-roller-coaster.

**43.** Wedded Wonderland. "This Is What Happens If You're Single in These 7 Countries." *Wedded Wonderland,* October 4, 2023, https://weddedwonderland.com/this-is-what-happens-if-youre-single-in-these-7-countries.

**44.** Wood, Alex M., Alex P. Linley, et al. "The Authentic Personality: A Theoretical and Empirical Conceptualization and the Development of the Authenticity Scale." *Journal of Counseling Psychology.* (2008), 55(3), 385–399, https://doi.org/10.1037/0022-0167.55.3.385.

**45.** Zenger, Jack, and Joseph Folkman. "Research: Women Score Higher Than Men in Most Leadership Skills." *Harvard Business Review,* June 25, 2019, https://hbr.org/2019/06/research-women-score-higher-than-men-in-most-leadership-skills.

**46.** Zoellner, Tom. *The Heartless Stone: A Journey Through the World of Diamonds, Deceit, and Desire.* New York: Picador, 2007.

# Notes

## INTRODUCTION

1.  Christine Kininmonth, "Adam Alter's 'Anatomy of a Break-through' Summary," *The Growth Faculty* (June 21, 2023), www.thegrowthfaculty.com/blog/adamalteranatomyofbreakthrough.

2.  Monica Potts, "Are Americans Unhappy?," *FiveThirtyEight* (March 28, 2022), https://fivethirtyeight.com/features/are-americans-unhappy/.

3.  Scott Anderson, "The Correlation Between Change Management and Project Success," *Prosci* (blog), (updated October 2, 2023) www.prosci.com/blog/the-correlation-between-change-management-and-project-success.

## CHAPTER 1

1.  Jeff Kauflin, "Only 15% of People Are Self-Aware—Here's How to Change," *Forbes* (May 10, 2017), https://www.forbes.com/sites/jeffkauflin/2017/05/10/only-15-of-people-are-self-aware-heres-how-to-change/?sh=3a917c952b8c.

## CHAPTER 2

1.  Emily L. Loeb, Jessica Kansky, et al., "Perceived Psychological Control in Early Adolescence Predicts Lower Levels of Adaptation into Mid-Adulthood," *Child Development* (2021), 92(2), e158–e172, doi:10.1111/cdev.13377.

2.   Prince Harry, the Duke of Sussex, *Spare* (New York: Random House, 2023), 23–25.

3.   Karl Pillemer, PhD, *Fault Lines: Fractured Families and How to Mend Them* (New York: Avery, 2022).

## CHAPTER 3

1.   Jeffrey M. Jones, "U.S. Church Membership Falls Below Majority for First Time," *Gallup* (March 29, 2021), https://news.gallup.com/poll/341963/church-membership-falls-below-majority-first-time.aspx.

2.   Henri Tajfel, M.G. Billig, et al., "Social Categorization and Intergroup Behaviour," *European Journal of Social Psychology* (1971), 1(2), 149–178, https://doi.org/10.1002/ejsp.2420010202.

3.   Pew Research Center, "Religious Landscape Study," *Pew Research Center* (2014), www.pewresearch.org/religion/religious-landscape-study/views-about-homosexuality.

## CHAPTER 4

1.   Jared Wadley, "Men, Women Ride the Same Emotional Roller Coaster," *University of Michigan News* (October 25, 2021), https://news.umich.edu/men-women-ride-the-same-emotional-roller-coaster.

2.   John D. Rich, Jr., PhD, "Strict Gender Roles Hurt Men, Too," *Psychology Today* (blog) (March 21, 2018), www.psychologytoday.com/us/blog/parenting-purpose/201803/strict-gender-roles-hurt-men-too.

3.   Centers for Disease Control and Prevention, "Suicide Data and Statistics," *CDC.gov* (April 6, 2023), www.cdc.gov/suicide/suicide-data-statistics.html.

4. Christine Lagarde and Jonathan D. Ostry, "When More Women Join the Workforce, Everyone Benefits. Here's Why," *World Economic Forum* (December 4, 2018), www.weforum.org/agenda/2018/12/economic-gains-from-gender-inclusion-even-greater-than-you-thought.

5. Megan Leonhardt, "American Women Are Increasingly the Breadwinner. But Many Are Still in Charge of Childcare, Cooking, and Cleaning," *Fortune* (April 13, 2023), https://fortune.com/2023/04/13/more-american-women-becoming-breadwinners/.

6. Laura Vanderkam, "Why Offering Paid Maternity Leave Is Good for Business," *Fast Company* (September 27, 2016), www.fastcompany.com/3064070/why-offering-paid-maternity-leave-is-good-for-business.

7. Jack Zenger and Joseph Folkman, "Research: Women Score Higher Than Men in Most Leadership Skills," *Harvard Business Review* (June 25, 2019), https://hbr.org/2019/06/research-women-score-higher-than-men-in-most-leadership-skills.

8. Rachel Bowley, "Women's Equality Day: A Look at Women in the Workplace in 2017," *LinkedIn Official Blogs* (blog) (August 28, 2017), https://blog.linkedin.com/2017/august/28/womens-equality-day-a-look-at-women-in-the-workplace-in-2017.

9. Molly Ringwald, "What About 'The Breakfast Club'?," *The New Yorker* (April 6, 2018), www.newyorker.com/culture/personal-history/what-about-the-breakfast-club-molly-ringwald-metoo-john-hughes-pretty-in-pink.

## CHAPTER 5

1. U.S. Surgeon General, "Our Epidemic of Loneliness and Isolation," (2023), www.hhs.gov/sites/default/files/surgeon-general-social-connection-advisory.pdf, p. 24.

2. Fons Trompenaars and Charles Hampden-Turner, *Riding the Waves of Culture: Understanding Diversity in Global Business* (Boston: Nicholas Brealey Publishing, 2020).

## CHAPTER 6

1. Wedded Wonderland, "This Is What Happens If You're Single in These 7 Countries," *Wedded Wonderland* (October 4, 2023), https://weddedwonderland.com/this-is-what-happens-if-youre-single-in-these-7-countries.

2. Bella DePaolo, PhD, "Why So Many Women Are Perfectly Happy to Stay Single," *Psychology Today* (blog) (October 29, 2018), www.psychologytoday.com/us/blog/living-single/201810/why-so-many-women-are-perfectly-happy-to-stay-single.

3. Maude Bass-Kreuger, "Everything You Ever Wanted to Know About the White Wedding Dress," *Vogue* (July 22, 2020), www.vogue.co.uk/gallery/history-of-the-white-wedding-dress.

4. Tom Zoellner, *The Heartless Stone: A Journey Through the World of Diamonds, Deceit, and Desire* (New York: Picador, 2007).

5. Reuters, "Husbands Create 7 Hours of Extra Housework for Their Wives," *Huffington Post* (February 19, 2016), www.huffpost.com/entry/husbands-create-7-hours-of-extra-housework-for-their-wives_n_56c72146e4b0ec6725e23e2c.

6. PRB, "Research Shows Moms with Husbands or Live-In Male Partners Do More Housework Than Single Moms." *PRB* (May 8, 2019), www.prb.org/news/mothers-day.

7. Dr. Darcy Lockman, "What 'Good' Dads Get Away With," *The New York Times* (May 4, 2019), www.nytimes.com/2019/05/04/opinion/sunday/men-parenting.html.

8. Taylor Orth, "Does Society Pressure Men and Women to Have Children?," *YouGov* (February 8, 2022), https://today.yougov.com/topics/politics/articles-reports/2022/02/08/does-society-pressure-men-and-women-have-children.

9. Stephanie Kirchgaessner, "Pope Francis: Not Having Children Is Selfish," *The Guardian* (February 11, 2015), www.theguardian.com/world/2015/feb/11/pope-francis-the-choice-to-not-have-children-is-selfish.

10. Statista Research Department, "Percentage of Childless Women in the United States in 2020, By Age," *Statista* (June 2, 2023), hwww.statista.com/statistics/241535/percentage-of-childless-women-in-the-us-by-age/#:~:text=In%202020%2C%2097.2%20percent%20of,44%20years%20old%20were%20childless.

11. Dr. Shaheena Janiuha-Jivraj, "The Daddy Dilemma, Why Fatherhood Is Still a Penalty for Men's Careers," *Forbes* (May 16, 2023), www.forbes.com/sites/shaheenajanjuhajivrajeurope/2023/05/16/the-daddy-dilemma-why-fatherhood-is-still-a-penalty-for-mens-careers/?sh=33c074b841bc.

12. Ben Renner, "Fathers Today More Engaged with Their Kids 'Than Ever Before,' Study Finds," *StudyFinds* (June 19, 2022), https://studyfinds.org/fathers-more-engaged-with-kids-than-ever-before.

13. Joanna Pocock, "Not So Lonely: Busting the Myth of the Only Child," *JSTOR Daily* (November 8, 2015), https://daily.jstor.org/myth-lonely-only-child.

## CHAPTER 7

1. Gettysburg College, "One Third of Your Life Is Spent at Work," *Gettysburg College*, www.gettysburg.edu/news/stories?id=79db7b34-630c-4f49-ad32-4ab9ea48e72b.

2. Lori Amato, "What Is the Average Number of Career Changes in a Person's Lifetime?," *Unmudl* (April 4, 2023), https://unmudl.com/blog/average-career-changes.

3. Gili Malinsky, "'Work Is the Most Important Way of Proving Your Worth,' and It's Making Americans Miserable: Professor," *CNBC* (January 26, 2022), www.cnbc.com/2022/01/26/work-is-the-most-important-way-of-proving-your-worth-in-the-us-says-professor.html.

## CHAPTER 8

1. Itamar Shatz, PhD, "The Value-Action Gap: Why People Don't Act in Accordance with Their Beliefs," *Effectiviology*, https://effectiviology.com/value-action-gap.

2. Kenneth M. Sheldon, Andrew J. Elliot, et al., "Self-Concordance and Subjective Well-Being in Four Cultures," *Journal of Cross-Cultural Psychology* (2004), 35(2), 209–223, https://doi.org/10.1177/0022022103262245.

3. Alex M. Wood, Alex P. Linley, et al., "The Authentic Personality: A Theoretical and Empirical Conceptualization and the Development of the Authenticity Scale," *Journal of Counseling Psychology* (2008), 55(3), 385–399, https://doi.org/10.1037/0022-0167.55.3.385. Kenneth M. Sheldon, Richard M. Ryan, et al., "Trait Self and True Self: Cross-Role Variation in the Big-Five Personality Traits and Its Relations with Psychological Authenticity and Subjective Well-Being," *Journal of Personality and Social Psychology* (1997), 73(6), 1380–1393, https://doi.org/10.1037/0022-3514.73.6.1380.

## CHAPTER 10

1. Nap Ministry, "Rest Is Resistance: A Manifesto," *The Nap Ministry*, https://thenapministry.com.

2.  David Neal, Wendy Wood, and Jeffrey Quinn, "Habits—A Repeat Performance," *Current Directions in Psychological Science* (2006), 15(4), https://doi.org/10.1111/j.1467-8721.2006.00435.x.

3.  James Clear, "How to Build a New Habit: This Is Your Strategy Guide," *JamesClear.com*, https://jamesclear.com/habit-guide; Alex Janin, "The New Science on Making Healthy Habits Stock," *The Wall Street Journal* (September 27, 2023), www.wsj.com/health/wellness/healthy-habits-research-science-7f373f67.

4.  Naz Beshesti, "Toxic Influence: An Average of 80% of Americans Have Experienced Emotional Abuse," *Forbes* (May 15, 2020), www.forbes.com/sites/nazbeheshti/2020/05/15/an-average-of-80-of-americans-have-experienced-emotional-abuse/?sh=3da74d697b49.

5.  Julianne Holt-Lunstad, Timothy B. Smith, J. Bradley Layton, "Social Relationships and Mortality Risk: A Meta-Analytic Review," *PLoS Medicine* (2010), 7(7), e1000316. doi:10.1371/journal.pmed.1000316.

6.  Sheldon Cohen, William J. Doyle, et al., "Sociability and Susceptibility to the Common Cold," *Psychological Science* (2003), 14(5), 389–395, https://doi.org/10.1111/1467-9280.01452.

# About the Authors

**KERI OHLRICH, PHD** has more than twenty years of experience on the front lines of Human Resources, working in leadership positions at a variety of organizations, from startups to Fortune 500 companies. As cofounder of Abbracci Group and coauthor of *The Way of the HR Warrior*, she continues her mission to share insights from these experiences with others who are passionate about HR excellence. She cohosts *The Breakout* podcast to get advice and insights from people breaking free from expectations and shares her experience as a regular guest on many other podcasts, in industry interviews and articles, as well as speaking engagements in the US and abroad. She is an iPEC Certified Professional Coach (CPC), as well as a certified Prosci® change management practitioner along with a variety of personality and cultural assessments, including Caliper, iPEC Energy Leadership Index (ELI), and the Denison Cultural Assessment.

**KELLY GUENTHER** is cofounder of Abbracci Group and cohost of *The Breakout* podcast, in which she brings a holistic approach to HR, focusing not only on the organization but also on the individuals who create the team. She has led sales training programs and certification processes for over 500 VPs, sales executives, and branch managers. Her passion for and commitment to delivering exceptional results has proudly earned her trusted advisor status with her clients. She is an iPEC Certified Professional Coach (CPC), as well as a certified Prosci® change management practitioner along with a variety of personality assessments, including Caliper, iPEC Energy Leadership Index (ELI), and Myers-Briggs Type Indicator (MBTI).